COASTAL NEW ENGLAND SPRING COOKING

Second Edition

By
Sherri Eldridge

Illustrations by
Robert Groves
Nadine Pranckunas

The gratitude of the author is extended to the Maine Chapter of the American Heart Association for the guidance and information provided. The use of the Association's name to convey the goals of this series of books is also gratefully appreciated. For each book sold the publisher makes a contribution to the American Heart Association to further their life-preserving efforts of research and education.

Coastal New England Spring Cooking
by Sherri Eldridge
Published by Harvest Hill Press

For additional copies of the cookbooks in this series:
Coastal New England Spring Cooking   *Coastal New England Winterfare & Holiday Cooking*
Coastal New England Summertime Cooking   *Coastal New England Fall Harvest Cooking*
send $13.95 per book (Maine residents add state sales tax) plus shipping of $2.00 for the first book and $1.00 for each additional book to the publisher:

Harvest Hill Press, P.O. Box 55, Salisbury Cove, Maine 04672
VISA and Master Card are accepted. Credit card orders may call (207) 288-8900.

ISBN: 1-886862-09-5 (Second Edition)   PRINTED IN THE U.S.A.

First Printing: March 1995
Second Printing: June 1995 (Revised)
Third Printing: September 1996
Fourth Printing: March 1998 (Second Edition)
Fifth Printing: August 1998

20% TOTAL RECYCLED FIBER
20% POST CONSUMER FIBER

PREFACE

The long-awaited glories of spring arrive with blades of new green grass, the beautiful blooming of the simple crocus, and the tender produce and herbs of this anticipated season. More than any other time of year, vegetables and berries are bursting with freshness and flavor. Spring in New England is cherished today as it has been for centuries. The people of this seaside region share a diversity of family origin and a common New England heritage, which combine to make this authentic coastal New England cuisine.

With the publication of this second edition, a nutritional analysis has been added to help meet your dietary goals. The American Heart Association has developed sound guidelines to assist in the prevention of heart disease, and living a long and healthy life. A pleasurable diet, low in fats and meats, and high in seasonally fresh vegetables, fruits, fishes and grains has also been shown to have numerous other health benefits.

These recipes have been adapted to meet the guidelines of the American Heart Association for healthy adults. Although all recipes are reduced in fat and cholesterol, those such as chocolate desserts should not be eaten every day, but enjoyed once or twice a week. A heart-healthy diet includes diverse and good-tasting dishes that are reasonably low in fat, served in average size proportions, employing common sense meal plans, and regular exercise.

The Hints and References section has specific guidelines for a heart-healthy diet. Also shown is data on the fats and cholesterol found in oils. Although the sodium and sugars in these recipes has been reduced or removed, people on strict diets should adapt recipes to their individual needs.

Please take a few minutes and explore the resources in this book. It has been carefully written to offer you the best of Coastal New England Cooking.

This book is dedicated to my mother-in-law,
Sis Eldridge,
and all good cooks,
who preserve their family recipes and history
for their children to cherish and enjoy.

The Coastal New England Cookbook Collection follows the American Heart Association Guidelines for Healthy Adults. These wonderful recipes will help make following the American Heart Association guidelines easier and more fun for you by supplying flavorful reduced fat/salt menu ideas using ingredients from your shelves.

...Beth Davis, R.D. M.Ed.

Beth Davis is a Registered Dietician and former member of the American Heart Association's Speaker's Bureau and Heart Health Education of the Young Task Force.

CREDITS:

Cover: "Les Jardin" daffodil print cotton, gratefully used as a courtesy of:
Hoffman International Fabrics

Cover Designs, Layout and Typesetting: Sherri Eldridge

Front Cover Nautical and Back Cover Watercolors, Chapter Title Page Art:
Robert Groves, Brooksville, Maine

Text Line Sketches: Robert Groves and Nadine Pranckunas

Proofreading: Bill Eldridge, Jerry Goldberg, Eleanor Rhinelander and Marcie Correa

Support, Patience and Recipes: Bill Eldridge, Fran Goldberg, The LeForestiers, Annie Shaw and the Women's Business Development Corporation

CONTENTS

Breakfast
and
Fresh Fruits

CONTENTS

For other breakfast foods, please refer to the chapters
"Breads and Baked Goods" and "Desserts and Sweets."

Strawberry-Lime Yogurt Shake

1 cup fresh or frozen
    strawberries
2 tablespoons frozen
    limeade concentrate
1 cup non-fat plain
    yogurt
2 tablespoons honey or
    sugar

Garnish:
mint sprigs, strawberries
    or lime wedges

SERVES 2

Wash, hull and halve strawberries. Put all ingredients, except the honey or sugar, in blender. Whip on medium speed 1 minute. Add honey or sugar, blend 20 seconds more.

Pour into serving glasses. Garnish with fresh mint sprigs, strawberries or lime wedges.

Serving: 1/2 Recipe	Calories: 163	Protein: 6 gm
Calories from Fat: 3	Total Fat: .5 gm	Dietary Fiber: 2 gm
Saturated Fat: 0 gm	Carbs: 37 gm	Sodium: 67 mg
Component of Fat: 1%	Cholesterol: 0 mg	Calcium: 162 mg

Spring Fruit Bowl & Berry Sauce

1 large or 2 small
    bananas
2 tablespoons honey or
    sugar
$1/2$ cup orange juice
1 quart fresh strawberries,
    cleaned and halved
1 cup fresh, or frozen and
    drained, raspberries
1 cup fresh or canned
    pineapple pieces,
    unsweetened
2 apples, cut in bite-sized
    pieces

SERVES 4

Chop banana into bite sized pieces. Place half of the banana pieces into blender with honey or sugar, orange juice, and $1/2$ cup of the strawberries. Blend 40 seconds.

Put all remaining fruit into serving bowl and lightly toss with blended sauce. Chill.

Serving: 1/4 Recipe
Calories from Fat: 12
Saturated Fat: 0 gm
Component of Fat: 5%

Calories: 201
Total Fat: 1.5 gm
Carbs: 50 gm
Cholesterol: 0 mg

Protein: 2 gm
Dietary Fiber: 8 gm
Sodium: 3 mg
Calcium: 40 mg

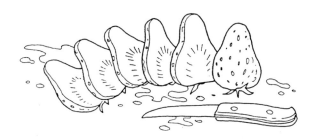

Apricot Compote

2 lbs. fresh apricots or
    peaches
1 orange
1 lemon
$\frac{1}{2}$ cup apple juice
$\frac{1}{2}$ cup light brown sugar
1 teaspoon vanilla
pinch of salt

SERVES 4

Place apricots in covered saucepan of boiling water. Blanch for 5 minutes. Remove from saucepan and set in ice water for 1 minute. The skins can now be easily removed.

Cut peeled apricots into bite-sized pieces, and put in large saucepan. Grate peel from orange and lemon into saucepan. Squeeze juice of orange and lemon and add to saucepan with remaining ingredients. Cover saucepan and cook over medium-high heat for 25 minutes. Delicious, served warm or chilled.

Serving: 1/4 Recipe	Calories: 201	Protein: 2 gm
Calories from Fat: 12	Total Fat: 1.5 gm	Dietary Fiber: 8 gm
Saturated Fat: 0 gm	Carbs: 50 gm	Sodium: 3 mg
Component of Fat: 5%	Cholesterol: 0 mg	Calcium: 40 mg

Poached Prunes and Fresh Fruits

3 cups water
1 cup dried pitted prunes
1 quart fresh or frozen
    peaches, pears, and/or
    apricots
$1/_2$ cup sugar
$1/_2$ teaspoon vanilla
    extract

MAKES 1 QUART

Boil water in large saucepan. Cut prunes into quarters, and fresh fruit into pieces. Add fruits to boiling water and reduce heat to medium. Simmer until fruit and skins are almost tender, about 20 minutes. Add sugar and vanilla, cook 5 minutes more.

Serving: 1/6 Recipe	Calories: 355	Protein: 4 gm
Calories from Fat: 8	Total Fat: 1 gm	Dietary Fiber: 2 gm
Saturated Fat: 0 gm	Carbs: 91 gm	Sodium: 12 mg
Component of Fat: 2%	Cholesterol: 0 mg	Calcium: 40 mg

Tips to Reduce Calories: By adding sugar late in the cooking process, you can use less sugar, and end up with the same degree of sweetness. If using a non-caloric sugar substitute instead of granulated sugar, use one-eighth teaspoon to replace 1 teaspoon sugar. Where possible, try substituting honey, maple syrup, brown sugar or molasses for sugar.

Perfect Pancakes

SERVES 4

1¹/₄ cups sifted, all-purpose
   flour
³/₄ cup whole grain flour
2 teaspoons baking powder
1 tablespoon sugar
1 egg
1 egg white
1 cup low-fat buttermilk
1 cup skim milk
1 tablespoon canola oil

Combine dry ingredients in a large bowl. In a separate bowl, whip eggs, then mix in other wet ingredients. Add liquid mixture to dry ingredients and mix slightly. Some lumps will remain. Cook on preheated griddle.

Serving: 1/4 Recipe	Calories: 319	Protein: 36 gm
Calories from Fat: 80	Total Fat: 9 gm	Dietary Fiber: 4 gm
Saturated Fat: 3.5 gm	Carbs: 52 gm	Sodium: 348 mg
Component of Fat: 18%	Cholesterol: 54 mg	Calcium: 253 mg

Cinnamon-Orange Maple Syrup

SERVES 4

1 cup maple syrup
1 teaspoon cornstarch
¹/₂ cup orange juice
4-inch cinnamon stick
¹/₂ teaspoon vanilla

Dissolve cornstarch in 4 tablespoons of the maple syrup. Stir into saucepan with remaining maple syrup, orange juice and cinnamon stick. Simmer until thickened. Remove from heat, add vanilla. Serve warm.

Serving: 1/4 Recipe	Calories: 212	Protein: 0 gm
Calories from Fat: 1	Total Fat: 0 gm	Dietary Fiber: 0 gm
Saturated Fat: 0 gm	Carbs: 54 gm	Sodium: 8 mg
Component of Fat: 0%	Cholesterol: 0 mg	Calcium: 84 mg

Corn Cakes

1 cup cornmeal
1 cup all-purpose flour
1 teaspoon baking powder
1 teaspoon cinnamon
2 cups low-fat buttermilk
1 egg, separated
1 egg white
1 teaspoon vanilla extract

SERVES 4

In a large bowl, sift together dry ingredients. In a separate bowl, beat buttermilk, egg yolk and vanilla. Briefly stir wet mixture into dry. Beat egg whites until soft peaks form, gently fold into batter. Spray pre-heated griddle with non-stick oil. Cook cakes on both sides.

Serving: 1/4 Recipe	Calories: 309	Protein: 58 gm
Calories from Fat: 77	Total Fat: 8.5 gm	Dietary Fiber: 4 gm
Saturated Fat: 5.5 gm	Carbs: 54 gm	Sodium: 301 mg
Component of Fat: 15%	Cholesterol: 54 mg	Calcium: 210 mg

Vanilla-Bean Honey

2 cups honey
$\frac{1}{2}$ cup water
2 teaspoons lemon zest
3 vanilla beans

MAKES 2 CUPS

Combine all ingredients in a saucepan. Bring mixture to a boil, then simmer 10 minutes. Remove vanilla beans. Serve warm.

Serving: 1/4 Cup	Calories: 256	Protein: 0 gm
Calories from Fat: 0	Total Fat: 0 gm	Dietary Fiber: 0 gm
Saturated Fat: 0 gm	Carbs: 69 gm	Sodium: 4 mg
Component of Fat: 0%	Cholesterol: 0 mg	Calcium: 6 mg

Buttermilk-Batter Waffles

SERVES 4

2 cups cake flour
2 teaspoons baking powder
1 tablespoon sugar
2 cups low-fat buttermilk
1/2 cup non-fat plain
    yogurt
2 eggs, separated

Sift together dry ingredients. In a separate bowl, whip buttermilk, yogurt and egg yolks. Briefly stir mixtures together, some lumps will remain. Beat egg whites to soft peaks, fold into batter. Cook in hot waffle iron.

Serving: 1/4 Recipe	Calories: 309	Protein: 59 gm
Calories from Fat: 85	Total Fat: 9.5 gm	Dietary Fiber: 0 gm
Saturated Fat: 6 gm	Carbs: 52 gm	Sodium: 419 mg
Component of Fat: 16%	Cholesterol: 107 mg	Calcium: 287 mg

Strawberry Butter

MAKES 2 CUPS

1 cup whipped butter,
    softened at room temp.
1/2 cup powdered sugar
1/2 teaspoon vanilla extract
1 pint strawberries, cleaned
    finely chopped

With a small whisk, blend powdered sugar and vanilla into butter. Mix in strawberries.

Serving: 2 Tablespoons	Calories: 56	Protein: 0 gm
Calories from Fat: 37	Total Fat: 4 gm	Dietary Fiber: 0 gm
Saturated Fat: 2.5 gm	Carbs: 5 gm	Sodium: 45 mg
Component of Fat: 64%	Cholesterol: 10 mg	Calcium: 3 mg

Whipped butter, with more air space in its volume, has almost 20% less fat per tablespoon than stick butter. The fat content can be further diluted with fruits, vegetables, honey or other low-fat ingredients. There are 11 grams of fat in 1 tablespoon of stick butter. The Strawberry Butter recipe above has only 2 grams of fat per tablespoon.

Orange French Toast

12 slices white toasting
    bread
4 eggs
3 egg whites
$^3/_4$ cup skim milk
$^1/_2$ cup orange juice
1 teaspoon vanilla extract
1 teaspoon cinnamon
1 teaspoon nutmeg
1 tablespoon canola oil for
    frying

MAKES 12 SLICES

Trim crust off bread. In a large mixing bowl, combine all other ingredients, except oil, and beat well. Soak each slice of bread in the egg mixture for 1 minute. Stack bread after dipping, and then repeat dipping process.

Spray frying pan with non-stick vegetable oil, and cover with thin coat of canola oil. Fry French toast on medium-high heat until golden brown on each side.

Serving: 2 Slices	Calories: 233	Protein: 11 gm
Calories from Fat: 71	Total Fat: 8 gm	Dietary Fiber: 2 gm
Saturated Fat: 2 gm	Carbs: 29 gm	Sodium: 344 mg
Component of Fat: 31%	Cholesterol: 142 mg	Calcium: 128 mg

Raspberry Yogurt Whip

MAKES $2^1/_2$ CUPS

1 cup raspberries
1 cup non-fat vanilla
    yogurt
2 egg whites
$^1/_2$ cup sugar

Mix raspberries into yogurt. In a separate bowl beat egg whites, gradually adding sugar, until stiff. Fold egg whites into yogurt.

Serving: 1/6 Recipe	Calories: 233	Protein: 11 gm
Calories from Fat: 71	Total Fat: 8 gm	Dietary Fiber: 2 gm
Saturated Fat: 2 gm	Carbs: 29 gm	Sodium: 344 mg
Component of Fat: 31%	Cholesterol: 142 mg	Calcium: 128 mg

Eggs Benedict with Smoked Salmon

8 eggs
2 oz. sliced smoked salmon
$^3/_4$ cup water
1 tablespoon cornstarch
2 tablespoons lemon juice
pinch of cayenne
$^1/_2$ teaspoon white pepper
2 egg yolks
2 teaspoons unsalted butter
4 English muffins

To Serve: Toast muffins. On each half place a slice of smoked salmon and a hot poached egg. Cover with 2 tablespoons hollandaise.

SERVES 4

Eggs: In a small pot boil 4 inches of slightly salted water. Crack an egg open, swirl water with wooden spoon, and drop egg in center of swirl. Reduce heat, cook 4 minutes. Remove egg, plunge in cold water. Repeat process for other eggs. Just before serving, reheat eggs 2 minutes in hot (not boiling) water.

Hollandaise: Boil water in lower pan of a double boiler. In the top pan, whisk $^3/_4$ cup water, cornstarch, lemon juice and spices. Stirring constantly,   simmer 3 minutes. Remove from heat and whisk in 2 egg yolks and butter. Return to top of double boiler, stir and cook 3 minutes, or until thickened.

Serving: 1/4 Recipe	Calories: 358	Protein: 21 gm
Calories from Fat: 147	Total Fat: 16.5 gm	Dietary Fiber: 2 gm
Saturated Fat: 5.5 gm	Carbs: 30 gm	Sodium: 505 mg
Component of Fat: 42%	Cholesterol: 539 mg	Calcium: 164 mg

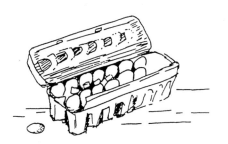

Camden Lobster Omelette

2 oz. cooked lobster meat
1 tablespoon dry white
$\frac{1}{4}$ teaspoon butter
1 large egg
1 egg white
1 teaspoon water
fresh ground pepper

Note: Have spatula handy to assist omelette through its formative stages. It will be cooked in 30 seconds!

MAKES ONE OMELETTE
Multiply ingredients by number of omelettes.

Cut lobster into small pieces, then sauté with wine and butter. Keep warm.

Preheat 8-10 inch, non-stick omelette pan over medium-high heat.

Whisk egg, egg white, water, salt and pepper together in bowl. Just before pouring eggs into pan, spray with non-stick oil. Pour eggs into middle of pan ($\frac{1}{2}$ cup at a time if using a number of eggs.) Shake and swirl pan to distribute eggs. Let rest 5 seconds to firm the bottom, while spreading lobster over the top.

Holding the pan by its handle, quickly jerk towards you while tilting far edge over burner. Continue this process and omelette will roll over on itself. When rolled omelette forms at far end, bang handle near pan to curl edge.

Serving: 1 Omelette	Calories: 166	Protein: 21 gm
Calories from Fat: 57	Total Fat: 6.5 gm	Dietary Fiber: 0 gm
Saturated Fat: 2 gm	Carbs: 2 gm	Sodium: 345 mg
Component of Fat: 36%	Cholesterol: 255 mg	Calcium: 63 mg

Strawberry-Rhubarb Jelly Rolls

2 cups all-purpose flour
2 teaspoons baking
    powder
2 teaspoons sugar
2 cups skim milk
3 large eggs
2 tablespoons canola oil
1 cup fresh strawberries,
    cleaned and cut into
    small pieces
$^1/_2$ cup rhubarb stalks,
    finely diced
$^1/_2$ cup sugar
1 tablespoon water
2 teaspoons cornstarch
1 teaspoon vanilla extract
$^1/_2$ teaspoon lemon juice

MAKES EIGHT 8-INCH JELLY ROLLS

Sift flour before measuring, then mix with baking powder and 2 teaspoons sugar. Whisk in milk, eggs and oil. Blend until perfectly smooth. Cover and rest in the refrigerator, at least 30 minutes, but preferably 1 hour.

Simmer strawberries, rhubarb and $^1/_2$ cup sugar in covered saucepan for 15 minutes. Blend water with cornstarch, then stir into strawberries and rhubarb. Cook until thickened, then stir in vanilla and lemon juice. Keep warm on very low heat until ready to roll up in the jelly rolls.

Preheat 8-inch crepe pan over medium-high heat. Spray with 2 coats of non-stick cooking oil and quickly pour $^1/_3$ cup batter into middle of pan, tilt to cover. After 1 minute, flip and cook 30 seconds on second side.

To Serve: Roll each jelly roll with 2 tablespoons of fruit sauce. Sprinkle tops with powdered sugar.

Serving: 1 Jelly Roll	Calories: 239	Protein: 7 gm
Calories from Fat: 47	Total Fat: 5 gm	Dietary Fiber: 1 gm
Saturated Fat: 1 gm	Carbs: 41 gm	Sodium: 149 mg
Component of Fat: 20%	Cholesterol: 54 mg	Calcium: 138 mg

Hot Rice Pudding with Raisins

4 cups skim milk
1 cup skimmed
    evaporated milk
1 cup uncooked short or
    medium-grain rice
pinch of salt
1 tablespoon butter
2 teaspoons vanilla
4 tablespoons sugar
1 cup golden raisins
2 teaspoons cinnamon

SERVES 6

Blend milks together and scald in a saucepan.

Boil water in lower pan of double boiler. Pour scalded milks into the top pan of the double boiler. Add rice and salt. Cook 1 hour over boiling water, allowing rice to soften and thicken. Stir frequently, and check to be sure water in bottom pan does not boil off.

Remove from heat while rice is still moist. Add butter, vanilla, 2 tablespoons sugar and raisins. Place warm pudding in serving dish or custard cups. Mix remaining sugar with cinnamon and sprinkle over the top.

Serving: 1/6 Recipe	Calories: 337	Protein: 12 gm
Calories from Fat: 25	Total Fat: 3 gm	Dietary Fiber: 2 gm
Saturated Fat: 1.5 gm	Carbs: 67 gm	Sodium: 177 mg
Component of Fat: 7%	Cholesterol: 10 mg	Calcium: 349 mg

Early New England homemakers had few means of decorating. To cheer up the homestead women created wall stencils, which became New England's first folk art. The stencils were made by repeating geometric shapes in soft colors. The earliest stencils of the 1700's were simple border designs, but complex wall patterns soon followed.

Hash Brown Potatoes

5 cups peeled and finely
  diced potatoes
1 tablespoon olive oil
1 cup onion, diced
2 cloves garlic, minced
1 tablespoon butter
1 tablespoon fresh or
  powdered sage
$^1/_2$ cup fresh chopped
  parsley
$^1/_2$ teaspoon salt
$^1/_2$ teaspoon ground black
  pepper

SERVES 4

Put potatoes in a large pot, cover with water and boil for 10 minutes.

Spray a large pan with non-stick oil. Sauté onion and garlic in olive oil until onions are clear. Add butter, and after it melts, put in the potatoes. Turn only as needed to keep from burning, scraping any sticking bits from bottom of pan. If needed, add a little extra olive oil. When potatoes are lightly golden, add sage and parsley, and continue frying until browned. Sprinkle with salt and pepper before serving.

Serving: 1/4 Recipe	Calories: 319	Protein: 7 gm
Calories from Fat: 63	Total Fat: 7 gm	Dietary Fiber: 6 gm
Saturated Fat: 2.5 gm	Carbs: 59 gm	Sodium: 346 mg
Component of Fat: 19%	Cholesterol: 8 mg	Calcium: 56 mg

Apple-Pecan Oatmeal

There is nothing so tasty as a bowl of old-fashioned, whole rolled oats.

$2^3/_4$ cups water
pinch of salt
1 cup whole rolled oats
2 tablespoons chopped
　　dried apples
2 tablespoons broken
　　pecan pieces

SERVES 2

Boil water and salt. Add rolled oats. Stirring occasionally, cook until water is absorbed. Remove from heat, and let set 5 minutes.

Sprinkle bowls of oatmeal with 1 tablespoon chopped dried apples and 1 tablespoon pecans. Serve with cinnamon and honey.

Serving: 1/2 Recipe	Calories: 214	Protein: 7 gm
Calories from Fat: 64	Total Fat: 7 gm	Dietary Fiber: 5 gm
Saturated Fat: 1 gm	Carbs: 32 gm	Sodium: 74 mg
Component of Fat: 29%	Cholesterol: 0 mg	Calcium: 31 mg

Breads
and
Baked Goods

CONTENTS

Sweet baked goods are also in the chapter "Desserts and Sweets."
Spreads for bread are located in "Appetizers and Finger Food."

Note: The nutritional analysis for breads is based on 12 slices per bread loaf.

Spiced Banana Bran Muffins

1³/₄ cups sifted all-
    purpose flour
¹/₄ teaspoon salt
¹/₃ cup sugar
2 teaspoons double-acting
    baking powder
1 tablespoon cinnamon
¹/₂ teaspoon ground cloves
¹/₂ cup bran flakes
2 eggs
2 tablespoons canola oil
1 teaspoon vanilla
¹/₂ cup skim milk
³/₄ cup mashed banana

MAKES 12 MUFFINS

Preheat oven to 400°. Spray muffin tins with non-stick vegetable oil.

Mix together all dry ingredients. In a separate bowl, beat eggs, then mix in remaining liquid ingredients. Combine the dry and liquid mixtures with just a few swift strokes.

Fill muffin tins two-thirds full. Bake until toothpick inserted in center of muffins comes out clean, about 20-25 minutes.

Serving: 1 Muffin	Calories: 141	Protein: 3 gm
Calories from Fat: 31	Total Fat: 3.5 gm	Dietary Fiber: 1 gm
Saturated Fat: .5 gm	Carbs: 24 gm	Sodium: 145 mg
Component of Fat: 22%	Cholesterol: 36 mg	Calcium: 56 mg

Cranberry-Nut Muffins

1³/₄ cups sifted all-purpose
  flour
¹/₄ teaspoon salt
²/₃ cup sugar
2 teaspoons double-acting
  baking powder
2 eggs
1¹/₂ tablespoons canola oil
1 teaspoon vanilla
¹/₃ cup skim milk
1 cup finely chopped
  cranberries, mixed with
  3 tablespoons sugar
¹/₄ cup chopped nutmeats
1 teaspoon finely grated
  orange rind

MAKES 12 MUFFINS

Preheat oven to 400°. Spray muffin tins with non-stick vegetable oil.

Sift together all dry ingredients. In a separate bowl, beat eggs, oil, vanilla and milk. Briefly stir together both mixtures. Add chopped cranberries, nuts and orange rind with a few swift strokes. Do not overmix.

Fill muffin tins two-thirds full. Bake about 25 minutes, or until toothpick inserted in center of muffins comes out clean.

Serving: 1 Muffin   Calories: 167   Protein: 3 gm
Calories from Fat: 38   Total Fat: 4 gm   Dietary Fiber: 1 gm
Saturated Fat: .5 gm   Carbs: 29 gm   Sodium: 130 mg
Component of Fat: 22%   Cholesterol: 35 mg   Calcium: 44 mg

Oatmeal-Blueberry Muffins

1 cup blueberries,
    preferably small
    wild blueberries
2 tablespoons flour
1 egg
$\frac{1}{2}$ cup brown sugar
2 tablespoons canola oil
$\frac{1}{2}$ cup skim milk
$\frac{1}{2}$ teaspoon vanilla
1 cup quick, uncooked
    oatmeal
2 teaspoons double-acting
    baking powder
1 cup all-purpose flour

MAKES 12 MUFFINS

Preheat oven to 400°. Spray muffin tins with non-stick vegetable oil. Drain blueberries well, then toss in 2 tablespoons flour to coat.

In a mixing bowl, beat egg, sugar, oil, vanilla and milk. With a few swift strokes, fold in remaining ingredients, then the blueberries.

Fill muffin tins two-thirds full. Bake for 20-25 minutes, or until toothpick inserted in center of muffins comes out clean.

Serving: 1 Muffin	Calories: 137	Protein: 3 gm
Calories from Fat: 30	Total Fat: 3.5 gm	Dietary Fiber: 1 gm
Saturated Fat: .5 gm	Carbs: 24 gm	Sodium: 82 mg
Component of Fat: 22%	Cholesterol: 18 mg	Calcium: 57 mg

The small Wild Blueberries of Maine are famous for their sweet blueberry-rich flavor. "Blueberry barrens" have shallow, sandy soils, located between large boulders deposited by glaciers. These fields were created by the same glaciers that are responsible for making Maine's granite coastline a jagged range of promontories, inlets and islands.

Buttermilk Biscuits

2 cups unbleached flour
1 tablespoon sugar
1 tablespoon baking
    powder
1 teaspoon baking soda
1 cup low-fat buttermilk
1 tablespoon canola oil

MAKES 12 BISCUITS

Preheat oven to 425°. Spray cookie sheet with non-stick vegetable oil.

Mix together all dry ingredients. With a fork, stir in the wet ingredients just until flour is moistened.

Drop biscuit dough by the tablespoon onto cookie sheet. Bake on middle rack for 10-12 minutes. Serve hot from the oven.

Serving: 1 Biscuit	Calories: 92	Protein: 10 gm
Calories from Fat: 22	Total Fat: 2.5 gm	Dietary Fiber: 1 gm
Saturated Fat: 1 gm	Carbs: 16 gm	Sodium: 234 mg
Component of Fat: 17%	Cholesterol: 0 mg	Calcium: 69 mg

Dinner Rolls

These low-fat rolls are actually good with any meal.

1 cup skim milk
$^1/_2$ teaspoon salt
2 tablespoons sugar
$^1/_2$ cup 105°-110° water
1 pkg. active dry yeast
4-5 cups all-purpose flour

MAKES 30 ROLLS

Scald milk. Add salt and sugar. Cool to lukewarm, then combine with water and sprinkle yeast on top. Let sit 5 minutes, then mix well. Gradually add flour, turning out onto kneading board when necessary. Knead dough until smooth and elastic. Cover and let rise until almost double in bulk.

Lightly roll out dough to about a 1-inch thickness. Using biscuit cutter or floured rim of drinking glass, cut out rolls. You can also cut them into squares with a sharp knife.

Place on cookie sheet sprayed with non-stick vegetable oil. Let rise again until double in bulk. Bake 35-40 minutes in preheated 275° oven. Serve immediately, or wrap well and store in refrigerator or freezer. If reheating, let warm to room temperature, then place in 300° oven for 10 minutes. Serve piping hot.

Serving: 1 Roll	Calories: 77	Protein: 2 gm
Calories from Fat: 2	Total Fat: 0 gm	Dietary Fiber: 1 gm
Saturated Fat: 0 gm	Carbs: 16 gm	Sodium: 45 mg
Component of Fat: 2%	Cholesterol: 0 mg	Calcium: 14 mg

Popovers

Afternoon tea and popovers with strawberry jam are served May to October on the lawn of Jordan Pond House in Acadia National Park, Maine.

1³/₄ cups sifted flour
1 teaspoon salt
3 eggs
1³/₄ cups skim milk
1¹/₂ tablespoons melted
　butter

Note: Popover baking cups should be deeper than they are wide. Some custard cups can be a good substitute. Batter will be about the same consistency as thick heavy cream.

MAKES 12 POPOVERS

Preheat oven to 425°. If glass, cast-iron or earthenware popover pans are to be used, place in oven to heat. If using aluminum, lightly spray with non-stick vegetable oil.

In a mixing bowl, beat all ingredients with an electric beater until batter is very smooth. If popover pans were heated in oven, remove and spray with non-stick oil.

Fill cups a little less than half full. Bake for 35 minutes, without opening oven! If oven has a glass door, watch for popovers to turn a rich golden color. Best served warm with jam.

Serving: 1 Popover
Calories from Fat: 27
Saturated Fat: 1.5 gm
Component of Fat: 25%

Calories: 106
Total Fat: 3 gm
Carbs: 15 gm
Cholesterol: 58 mg

Protein: 5 gm
Dietary Fiber: 0 gm
Sodium: 244 mg
Calcium: 53 mg

Potato Sticks

MAKES 46 STICKS

1 cup coarsely mashed
　　fresh boiled potatoes
$^1/_4$ cup canola oil
2 cups low-fat buttermilk
1 pkg. active dry yeast
1 tablespoon sugar
2 eggs, beaten
1 teaspoon salt
$7^1/_2$ cups sifted all-
　　purpose flour
2 tablespoons skim milk
2 tablespoons poppy seeds

Combine coarsely mashed potatoes with oil. In a saucepan, heat buttermilk to 105°-110°. Sprinkle yeast on buttermilk, rest 5 minutes, then stir until yeast dissolves. Mix yeast mixture, sugar, eggs and salt into potatoes. Stir in 6 cups of flour, turn onto board and knead in the rest. Place dough in bowl sprayed with non-stick oil, turn to coat all sides, cover. Let rise until doubled in bulk. Punch down. Divide into 46 balls and roll into 9-inch lengths. Brush tops with milk and sprinkle with poppy seeds. Let rise to double in bulk. Bake in preheated 425° oven for 15-18 minutes.

Serving: 2 Sticks	Calories: 189	Protein: 14 gm
Calories from Fat: 42	Total Fat: 4.5 gm	Dietary Fiber: 1 gm
Saturated Fat: 1.5 gm	Carbs: 32 gm	Sodium: 138 mg
Component of Fat: 19%	Cholesterol: 19 mg	Calcium: 49 mg

In the late 1840's, the Irish potato famine brought waves of Irish immigrants to Boston and New England. From 1820-1855, over 300,000 immigrants landed at Boston. All had traveled by sea in extremely rough conditions. More than half of the new immigrants were Irish, and just a short while later, they founded the Democratic party.

Quick Irish Soda Bread

2 cups all-purpose flour
2 teaspoons baking soda
2 teaspoons double-acting
  baking powder
2 tablespoons sugar
2 tablespoons butter
1 cup low-fat buttermilk
1/2 cup raisins
2 tablespoons caraway
  seeds
3 tablespoons skim milk

MAKES 8-INCH ROUND LOAF

Preheat oven to 350°. Spray a cookie sheet with non-stick vegetable oil.

In a mixing bowl, combine flour, baking soda, baking powder and sugar. Cut butter into flour mixture using a pastry cutter or two knives. Add buttermilk, raisins and caraway seeds, stirring just enough to combine.

Turn out onto floured surface and knead just 1 minute. Form into an 8-inch round loaf, place on prepared cookie sheet. Use a sharp knife to cut a bold cross over the top and sides, so crust will not crack while baking. Brush the top of loaf with milk. Bake 35 minutes on middle rack of oven.

Serving: 1 Slice
Calories from Fat: 31
Saturated Fat: 2 gm
Component of Fat: 19%

Calories: 127
Total Fat: 3.5 gm
Carbs: 23 gm
Cholesterol: 6 mg

Protein: 11 gm
Dietary Fiber: 1 gm
Sodium: 329 mg
Calcium: 70 mg

Basic Buttermilk Bread

$3^1/_2$ cups buttermilk
2 pkgs. active dry yeast
$^1/_2$ teaspoon baking soda
$^1/_2$ teaspoon salt
$^1/_4$ cup sugar
1 tablespoons melted
    butter
2 tablespoons canola oil
8 cups sifted unbleached
    flour
canola oil for brushing
    tops of loaves

MAKES THREE 9" x 5" LOAVES

Heat buttermilk to 110°, then sprinkle yeast on top. Let sit 5 minutes, then stir yeast until dissolved. Mix in baking soda, salt, sugar, butter and oil. Stir in as much flour as you can then turn out to knead in the rest.

Spray a large bowl with vegetable oil. Place dough in bowl, turning to coat all sides. Cover and let rise until double in bulk. Punch down, knead 2 minutes. Divide into 3 parts and shape into loaves. Place in bread pans sprayed with non-stick oil. Brush tops with oil. Let rise to double in bulk. Bake 45 minutes on middle rack of 400° oven.

Serving: 1 Slice	Calories: 120	Protein: 13 gm
Calories from Fat: 25	Total Fat: 3 gm	Dietary Fiber: 1 gm
Saturated Fat: 1.5 gm	Carbs: 22 gm	Sodium: 87 mg
Component of Fat: 15%	Cholesterol: 1 mg	Calcium: 34 mg

Honey Wheat Bread

$^1/_2$ cup 105°-115° water
2 pkgs. active dry yeast
1 egg, beaten
2 tablespoons safflower oil
$2^1/_4$ cups lukewarm water
$^1/_2$ teaspoon salt
$^3/_4$ cup honey
4 cups whole-wheat flour
4 cups all-purpose flour

MAKES THREE 5" x 9" LOAVES

Sprinkle yeast over 105°-115° water. Let sit 5 minutes, then stir until yeast is dissolved. Beat in all other ingredients, except flours.

Mix in whole-wheat flour, then all-purpose flour. Knead about 10 minutes, until dough is smooth and satiny. Place in bowl sprayed with non-stick oil, turn to coat all sides. Cover, set in warm place, and let rise until doubled in bulk. Punch dough down, knead again for 5 minutes. Shape into 3 loaves. Place in bread pans sprayed with non-stick oil. Set in warm place to rise until doubled in bulk. Bake 45 minutes in 350° oven.

Serving: 1 Slice	Calories: 123	Protein: 3 gm
Calories from Fat: 11	Total Fat: 1.5 gm	Dietary Fiber: 2 gm
Saturated Fat: 0 gm	Carbs: 25 gm	Sodium: 36 mg
Component of Fat: 9%	Cholesterol: 6 mg	Calcium: 8 mg

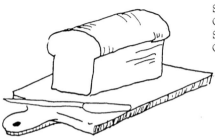

Herb Cheese Bread

1 cup warm water
2 pkgs. active dry yeast
1 tablespoon sugar
1 cup non-fat plain yogurt
1 cup skim milk
4 tablespoons olive oil
2 tablespoons rosemary
2 tablespoons basil
2 tablespoons dill
1 teaspoon salt
2 teaspoons black pepper
$^1/_2$ cup grated Parmesan
  cheese
8 cups unbleached flour

MAKES TWO 9" x 5" LOAVES

Combine water, yeast and sugar in mixing bowl, and let sit 10 minutes. Mix in yogurt, milk, oil, spices and cheese. Stir in as much flour as possible, then knead in the rest. Knead until smooth and elastic.

Place dough in a large bowl sprayed with non-stick oil, turn to coat all sides, then cover. Let rise in warm place until doubled in bulk. Punch down dough, knead 2 minutes. Shape into loaves. Place in bread pans sprayed with non-stick oil. Let rise until doubled in bulk. Bake on middle rack in preheated 350° oven for 45 minutes. Remove from pans and cool.

Serving: 1 Slice	Calories: 177	Protein: 5 gm
Calories from Fat: 26	Total Fat: 3 gm	Dietary Fiber: 1 gm
Saturated Fat: .5 gm	Carbs: 32 gm	Sodium: 125 mg
Component of Fat: 15%	Cholesterol: 1 mg	Calcium: 54 mg

Baked Boston Brown Bread

1 cup sifted all-purpose flour
2 tablespoons sugar
$\frac{1}{2}$ teaspoon salt
1 teaspoon baking soda
2 cups graham flour
1 cup low-fat buttermilk
1 cup dark molasses

Optional:
$\frac{3}{4}$ cup raisins

MAKES 9" x 5" LOAF

Preheat oven to 350°. Spray a 9" x 5" bread loaf pan with non-stick oil. Sift together flour, sugar, salt and baking soda. Stir in remaining ingredients in the order listed.

Pour into pan and bake 1 hour, or until toothpick inserted in center comes out clean.

Serving: 1 Slice
Calories from Fat: 14
Saturated Fat: 1 gm
Component of Fat: 6%

Calories: 178
Total Fat: 1.5 gm
Carbs: 40 gm
Cholesterol: 0 mg

Protein: 12 gm
Dietary Fiber: 3 gm
Sodium: 258 mg
Calcium: 220 mg

Original Boston Light Tower, First U.S. Lighthouse, Lighted 1716

Quick Carrot-Poppy Seed Bread

1½ cups grated carrots
¾ cup brown sugar
3 tablespoons honey
1 teaspoon lemon juice
1 teaspoon baking soda
2½ tablespoons safflower
    oil
3 tablespoons poppy seeds
1 cup boiling water
2 cups all-purpose flour
2 teaspoons baking
    powder
1 teaspoon cinnamon

MAKES ONE 9" x 5" LOAF

Preheat oven to 350°. Spray 9" x 5" bread pan with non-stick vegetable oil.

In a large mixing bowl, combine carrots, brown sugar, honey, lemon juice, baking soda, oil, poppy seeds and boiling water. Let rest at least 10 minutes.

In a separate bowl, mix flour, baking powder and cinnamon. After carrot mixture has rested, stir in flour mixture just until moistened (do not overmix). Pour into bread pan. Bake 40-50 minutes. When toothpick inserted in bread comes out clean, take out of oven. Leave in pan 10 minutes longer before removing from pan to cool on wire rack.

Serving: 1 Slice	Calories: 180	Protein: 3 gm
Calories from Fat: 36	Total Fat: 4 gm	Dietary Fiber: 1 gm
Saturated Fat: .5 gm	Carbs: 34 gm	Sodium: 183 mg
Component of Fat: 19%	Cholesterol: 0 mg	Calcium: 79 mg

Friendship Tea Ring

1 cup skim milk
$\frac{1}{4}$ cup canola oil
$\frac{1}{2}$ cup sugar
pinch of salt
2 pkgs. active dry yeast
$\frac{1}{4}$ cup very warm water
3 eggs
$5\frac{1}{2}$ cups all-purpose flour
$1\frac{1}{4}$ cups packed brown
    sugar
3 tablespoons cinnamon
2 cups finely chopped
    dried fruit: raisins,
    apricots and apples
$\frac{1}{4}$ cup chopped nuts
3 tablespoons skim milk
1 cup defrosted apple
    juice concentrate
1 tablespoon cinnamon,
    for top

MAKES 11-INCH BRAIDED RING

Scald milk, stir in oil, sugar and salt. In a small bowl stir yeast into water. In a large bowl, beat eggs, then add milk and yeast mixtures. Stir in flour, beat well. Turn onto lightly floured board and knead 5 minutes. Return to bowl, cover, put in warm place and let rise until doubled in bulk, about 2 hours.

Combine brown sugar, cinnamon, dried fruits and nuts. Roll dough into 12" x 22" rectangle, then cut into three 4" x 22" strips. Lay strips parallel on a cookie sheet, sprayed with non-stick oil. Spread fruit mixture down middle of each strip, roll edges to enclose fruit, seal seams with milk, and pinch ends. Gently braid strands, shape into ring, and tuck ends underneath. Cover, let rise until doubled in bulk. Boil juice concentrate until syrupy, then brush on ring and sprinkle with cinnamon. Bake in 350° oven 25 minutes.

Serving: 1/16 Recipe	Calories: 385	Protein: 7 gm
Calories from Fat: 55	Total Fat: 6 gm	Dietary Fiber: 3 gm
Saturated Fat: 1 gm	Carbs: 77 gm	Sodium: 43 mg
Component of Fat: 14%	Cholesterol: 40 mg	Calcium: 80 mg

Appetizers
and
Finger Food

CONTENTS

Appetizers can be used as a main dish by doubling the amount of food per serving.

Tomato, Basil and Sweet Pea Quiche

Pie Shell:
1½ cups non-fat cracker
    crumbs
2 tablespoons canola oil
2 tablespoons skim milk

Filling:
5 peeled tomatoes
1 tablespoon grated onion
1 teaspoon canola oil
¾ cup fresh sweet peas
3 eggs, beaten
1 cup skim milk
1 tablespoon fresh basil
1 teaspoon Worcestershire
    sauce
¾ cup grated low-fat
    Swiss Lorraine cheese

SERVES 6

Preheat oven to 375°. Spray a 9-inch pie plate with non-stick oil. Put crushed cracker crumbs in a mixing bowl. Sprinkle oil and milk over crumbs. Distribute moisture with a pastry cutter or fork. Press crumbs into pie plate and up the sides. Bake 5 minutes.

Cut tomatoes into bite-sized pieces, drain in sieve for 15 minutes, then gently press out liquid. Sauté onion in oil until nearly clear. Steam peas 5 minutes. Combine all filling ingredients in mixing bowl. Pour into pie shell. Bake 30 minutes or until golden.

Serving: 1/6 Recipe	Calories: 262	Protein: 13 gm
Calories from Fat: 82	Total Fat: 9 gm	Dietary Fiber: 3 gm
Saturated Fat: 1.5 gm	Carbs: 34 gm	Sodium: 109 mg
Component of Fat: 30%	Cholesterol: 112 mg	Calcium: 224 mg

Deviled Smoked Salmon

12 large eggs
$^1/_2$ cup non-fat sour cream
2 tablespoons lemon juice
$^1/_2$ teaspoon grated onion
$^1/_2$ teaspoon horseradish
$^1/_2$ teaspoon salt
$^1/_2$ teaspoon black pepper
$^1/_4$ lb. smoked salmon
1 tablespoon paprika

SERVES 12

Hard-boil eggs (about 7 minutes in boiling water). Peel and slice eggs in half lengthwise. Remove yolks, reserving 4 in a small mixing bowl, and discard remaining yolks.

Blend the 4 egg yolks with sour cream, lemon juice, onion, horseradish, salt and pepper. Cut or break apart smoked salmon into small pieces, then stir into mixture. Fill hollowed egg white halves with smoked salmon filling.

Sprinkle paprika over tops of deviled eggs. Arrange on platter with parsley or lettuce.

Serving: 1/12 Recipe	Calories: 71	Protein: 7 gm
Calories from Fat: 27	Total Fat: 3 gm	Dietary Fiber: 0 gm
Saturated Fat: 1 gm	Carbs: 3 gm	Sodium: 239 mg
Component of Fat: 39%	Cholesterol: 108 mg	Calcium: 29 mg

In the sixteenth and seventeenth centuries, large quantities of fish brought increasing numbers of Europeans to North America. The New England offshore banks, at just 200 feet deep, allow light to reach the ocean bottom, sustaining plants on which cod and haddock feed. Georges Bank, off Cape Cod, encompasses 10,000 square miles.

Scallop Puffs

$^1/_2$ lb. bay scallops
2 egg whites
$^1/_2$ cup grated low-fat
    Swiss Lorraine cheese
2 tablespoons low-fat
    mayonnaise
1 tablespoon grated onion
1 teaspoon paprika
$^1/_2$ teaspoon
    Worcestershire sauce
crackers or dried toast
    rounds

SERVES 4

Preheat broiler. Rinse scallops and briefly poach 5 minutes in boiling water. Drain well.

Beat egg whites until stiff. In a separate bowl, blend together Swiss Lorraine cheese, mayonnaise, onion and spices. Fold egg whites into cheese mixture, then scallops. Heap onto crackers or toast rounds. Set on cookie sheet to broil. Watch closely while broiling, remove when puffs are light golden brown. Serve hot.

Serving: 1/4 Recipe	Calories: 161	Protein: 20 gm
Calories from Fat: 38	Total Fat: 4 gm	Dietary Fiber: 1 gm
Saturated Fat: 1 gm	Carbs: 9 gm	Sodium: 319 mg
Component of Fat: 24%	Cholesterol: 35 mg	Calcium: 201 mg

(cont.) Fishing fleets came from France, England and Portugal to work the waters off the New England coast through the summer. They returned home in September with cod, mackerel and salmon for the European markets. Many New England coastal towns were founded as trading posts, selling supplies to service the ships and their crews.

Crab Spring Rolls

2 tablespoons vinegar
$1/2$ teaspoon sugar
1 tablespoon cornstarch
1 teaspoon Dijon mustard
2 garlic cloves, minced
8 oz. fresh crab meat
2 cups fresh bean sprouts
1 cup shredded Chinese
  cabbage
1 cup finely diced carrots
1 cup finely diced pepper
1 tablespoon grated onion
$1/2$ cup slivered water
  chestnuts
8 spring-roll or egg-roll
  wrappers
$1/2$ canola oil for frying

SERVES 8

Whisk vinegar and sugar together in a large mixing bowl. Stir in cornstarch, spices, crab, sprouts, cabbage, carrots, pepper, onion and water chestnuts.

Fill and roll spring-roll or egg-roll wrappers according to manufacturer's instructions. Pour canola oil into frying pan, heat on medium-high. It takes about 10 minutes before oil is hot enough. Carefully place spring rolls in hot oil, turning until browned on all sides (about 5-6 minutes). Drain on paper towels. If desired, serve with prepared sauce or tamari.

Serving: 1 Spring Roll	Calories: 136	Protein: 8 gm
Calories from Fat: 54	Total Fat: 6 gm	Dietary Fiber: 2 gm
Saturated Fat: .5 gm	Carbs: 14 gm	Sodium: 364 mg
Component of Fat: 38%	Cholesterol: 16 mg	Calcium: 49 mg

Steamed Mussels in White Wine

2 quarts mussels
1¹/₂ cups dry white wine
    or chardonnay
2 tablespoons chopped
    shallots
1 clove crushed garlic
1 tablespoon butter
pinch of salt
pinch of pepper

Serve with:
French bread

SERVES 4

Scrub mussels. Discard any that do not close tightly when cleaned.

In a large pot, bring wine, shallots, garlic and butter to a boil. Then add salt, pepper, and mussels, cover pot and steam until mussels open, about 12 minutes. Use a slotted spoon to scoop out mussels. Boil down broth until volume is reduced by half, then strain through a fine sieve to remove sand.

Serve mussels in individual bowls. Pour broth evenly over mussels in each bowl. Serve with a good French bread to dip in broth.

Serving: 1/4 Recipe	Calories: 153	Protein: 9 gm
Calories from Fat: 43	Total Fat: 4.5 gm	Dietary Fiber: 0 gm
Saturated Fat: 2 gm	Carbs: 4 gm	Sodium: 279 mg
Component of Fat: 28%	Cholesterol: 29 mg	Calcium: 30 mg

Cliff Walk
Newport, Rhode Island

Shrimp Cocktail

1 lb. large cooked shrimp,
   peeled and deveined
1 cup low-sodium chili
   sauce
1 teaspoon horseradish
1 tablespoon lemon juice
1 teaspoon Worcestershire
   sauce
1 tablespoon Madeira

Garnish:
lettuce leaves and
celery stalks

SERVES 4

Chill shrimp in refrigerator. Mix together remaining ingredients, blend well.

Line sherbet cups or small bowls with lettuce leaves. Spoon cocktail sauce into center of bowls. Hang shrimp from sides. Stick in celery stalks for garnish.

Serving: 1/4 Recipe
Calories from Fat: 13
Saturated Fat: .5 gm
Component of Fat: 7%

Calories: 185
Total Fat: 1.5 gm
Carbs: 15 gm
Cholesterol: 222 mg

Protein: 25 gm
Dietary Fiber: 0 gm
Sodium: 310 mg
Calcium: 59 mg

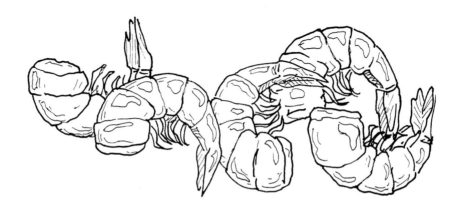

Mushroom Pâté

1 lb. fresh mushrooms
1 egg, separated
1 egg white
¹/₂ cup skimmed
    evaporated milk
1 small onion, grated
1 tablespoon soft butter
2 tablespoons brandy
1 teaspoon minced garlic
3 tablespoons finely
    chopped pecans
3 tablespoons flour
¹/₂ teaspoon salt
¹/₂ teaspoon white pepper

Serve with:
crackers

SERVES 6

Preheat oven to 325°. Spray small enamel or ceramic dish with non-stick oil. Set kettle of water to boil.

Process half the mushrooms in blender with egg yolk and milk until smooth. Chop remaining mushrooms very fine, then mix with remaining ingredients, except the egg whites. Beat egg whites until stiff. Lightly mix egg whites with both mushroom mixtures. Pour pâté into prepared dish and cover tightly with aluminum foil. Set pâté into larger baking dish. Pour boiling water into larger dish, half the depth of pâté dish. Bake 1-1¹/₂ hours until set. Chill.

Serving: 1/6 Recipe	Calories: 122	Protein: 6 gm
Calories from Fat: 50	Total Fat: 5.5 gm	Dietary Fiber: 2 gm
Saturated Fat: 2 gm	Carbs: 11 gm	Sodium: 262 mg
Component of Fat: 39%	Cholesterol: 42 mg	Calcium: 76 mg

Flaky Flounder Balls

1$^1/_2$ lbs. flounder fillets
4 medium potatoes,
    baked and scooped
    out of the skins
$^1/_3$ cup all-purpose flour
2 eggs
1 tablespoon canola oil
2 tablespoons low-fat
    buttermilk
1 tablespoon grated onion
1 teaspoon lemon juice
1 teaspoon minced garlic
salt and pepper to taste
skim milk for dipping
flour for dipping
$^1/_4$ cup canola oil for
    frying

SERVES 8

Process flounder through meat grinder or chop into tiny pieces. Rice or mash potatoes, then mix with flour, eggs, oil, buttermilk, onion, lemon juice and spices. Stir in flounder. Roll into 1-inch balls.

Spray frying pan with non-stick oil. Pour in oil and heat on medium-high. Dip flounder balls in milk, then roll in flour. Fry until light brown.

Presentation Suggestion: Serve Flaky Flounder Balls on toothpicks with Roquefort Pimento Dip (page 46).

Serving: 1/8 Recipe	Calories: 242	Protein: 22 gm
Calories from Fat: 71	Total Fat: 8 gm	Dietary Fiber: 1 gm
Saturated Fat: 1 gm	Carbs: 23 gm	Sodium: 111 mg
Component of Fat: 28%	Cholesterol: 94 mg	Calcium: 41 mg

By 1700 every coastal New England town was part of the fishing industry. Some fishermen worked the Banks, Ledges and Shoals nearest the coast and others ventured a few miles offshore. Rather than receive wages, the crew generally shared the profits of each day's catch. To this day, profit sharing has remained a standard of the fishing industry.

Spring Antipasto

2 tomatoes
1 cup sugar snap peas
1 cup fresh pole beans
1 cup fresh sliced peppers
1 cup fresh sliced carrots
8 black olives, sliced
4 oz. grated part-skim
    mozzarella cheese

SERVES 4

Slice tomatoes in rounds. Arrange vegetables in groupings on individual serving plates. Sprinkle sliced olives and grated mozzarella over all. Chill. Spoon about a tablespoon of Basil Pesto over antipasto before serving.

Serving: 1/4 Recipe	Calories: 155	Protein: 10 gm
Calories from Fat: 60	Total Fat: 6.5 gm	Dietary Fiber: 4 gm
Saturated Fat: 3 gm	Carbs: 16 gm	Sodium: 224 mg
Component of Fat: 37%	Cholesterol: 16 mg	Calcium: 229 mg

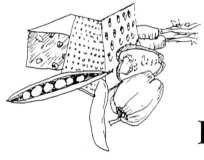

Basil Pesto

2 packed cups fresh basil
2 cloves peeled garlic
¼ cup toasted pine nuts
¼ cup grated Parmesan
1 tablespoon olive oil
2 teaspoons lemon juice

Wash, dry and stem basil leaves. In food processor or blender, drop in garlic cloves while machine is running, then drop in basil leaves, pine nuts and Parmesan. Stop motor and scrape down sides as needed. Process until smooth. Blend in oil and lemon juice.

Serving: 2 Tablespoons	Calories: 39	Protein: 2 gm
Calories from Fat: 30	Total Fat: 3.5 gm	Dietary Fiber: 0 gm
Saturated Fat: .5 gm	Carbs: 1 gm	Sodium: 32 mg
Component of Fat: 73%	Cholesterol: 1 mg	Calcium: 36 mg

Sour Cream Stuffed Mushrooms

1 lb. large cap mushrooms
1 cup non-fat sour cream
4 tablespoons grated
    Parmesan cheese
1 teaspoon dill
1 tablespoon chopped
    parsley
salt and pepper to taste
1 teaspoon finely chopped
    chives
paprika for tops

SERVES 4

Preheat broiler. Spray large baking dish with non-stick oil.

Gently pop stems out of mushroom caps. Chop stems into very small pieces, put in mixing bowl with sour cream, Parmesan, dill, parsley, salt and pepper. Chop inner white flesh of chive stalk and mix in.

With a small teaspoon, press stuffing into mushroom caps. Place in baking pan and sprinkle with paprika. On middle rack of oven, broil 10 minutes, or until lightly browned on top. Serve warm or chilled.

Serving: 1/4 Recipe	Calories: 126	Protein: 9 gm
Calories from Fat: 19	Total Fat: 2 gm	Dietary Fiber: 2 gm
Saturated Fat: 1 gm	Carbs: 18 gm	Sodium: 178 mg
Component of Fat: 15%	Cholesterol: 4 mg	Calcium: 168 mg

In recent years, grocery stores have made mushrooms a trusted item. Although a great many edible mushrooms grow wild in New England, characteristics of deadly species frequently mimic their safe cousins. Experienced mushroom hunters may find among the edible native species: chicken mushrooms, Morrel, giant Coprinus and "puff-balls."

Red Ribbon Sandwiches

8 oz. low-fat cream cheese
1 tablespoon non-fat
    sour cream
1 sweet red pepper
4 red radishes
1 teaspoon paprika
salt and pepper to taste
sliced white bread

SERVES 4

Allow cream cheese to soften at room temperature. Place in small mixing bowl and using fork, blend with sour cream. Dice red pepper into very small pieces and grate radishes. Add vegetables to mixing bowl with paprika, salt and pepper. Blend well. Adjust spices to taste.

Trim crust from bread. With a rolling pin, lightly roll bread slices, compacting to half the original thickness. Spread red cream on a slice, and cover with another slice of rolled bread. Cut sandwiches diagonally into 4 triangular pieces.

Serving: 1/4 Recipe   Calories: 188   Protein: 11 gm
Calories from Fat: 29   Total Fat: 3.5 gm   Dietary Fiber: 1 gm
Saturated Fat: 1 gm   Carbs: 28 gm   Sodium: 453 mg
Component of Fat: 16%   Cholesterol: 3 mg   Calcium: 64 mg

Roquefort Pimento Dip

1 cup non-fat plain
    yogurt
1 cup non-fat cottage
    cheese
$^1/_4$ cup Roquefort cheese
4 oz. jar sliced pimento,
    well drain
$^1/_2$ teaspoon pepper

MAKES $2^1/_3$ CUPS

Process yogurt and cottage cheese in blender until smooth. Crumble Roquefort into blender and whip. Pour into bowl, stir in drained pimento and pepper. Chill before serving with vegetable sticks.

Serving: 1/3 Cup	Calories: 58	Protein: 7 gm
Calories from Fat: 11	Total Fat: 1 gm	Dietary Fiber: 0 gm
Saturated Fat: 1 gm	Carbs: 4 gm	Sodium: 244 mg
Component of Fat: 20%	Cholesterol: 4 mg	Calcium: 93 mg

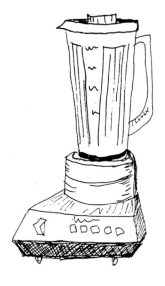

Olive Basil Dip

1 cup non-fat plain
    yogurt
1 cup non-fat cottage
    cheese
8 large pitted black olives
1 tablespoon pine nuts
$1/_2$ packed cup fresh basil
2 cloves crushed garlic
1 tablespoon lemon juice
2 tablespoons chopped
    parsley

MAKES $2^1/_2$ CUPS

Combine yogurt and cottage cheese in blender. Process until smooth. While blender is running, add remaining ingredients and blend until smooth. Transfer to serving bowl, cover, and chill at least 2 hours.

This dip is delicious with fresh vegetables, crackers or fish balls.

Serving: 1/2 Cup
Calories from Fat: 20
Saturated Fat: 0 gm
Component of Fat: 23%

Calories: 86
Total Fat: 2 gm
Carbs: 7 gm
Cholesterol: 1 mg

Protein: 9 gm
Dietary Fiber: 0 gm
Sodium: 256 mg
Calcium: 126 mg

Artichoke Spread

14 oz. can artichoke
    hearts
$^1/_2$ cup non-fat plain
    yogurt
4 oz. low-fat cream
    cheese, softened at
    room temperature
$^1/_2$ cup grated part-skim
    mozzarella cheese
1 teaspoon lemon juice
5 drops Tabasco sauce
$^1/_2$ teaspoon white pepper

SERVES 4

Drain artichokes, shaking out liquid from each artichoke heart. Chop into small pieces, press out moisture. Combine yogurt, cream cheese, mozzarella, lemon juice, Tabasco and pepper in blender. With blender running, add half of the chopped artichokes. Pour into bowl and mix in remaining artichoke pieces. Chill. Use as a dip or sandwich spread.

Serving: 1/4 Recipe	Calories: 64	Protein: 7 gm
Calories from Fat: 16	Total Fat: 2 gm	Dietary Fiber: 0 gm
Saturated Fat: 1 gm	Carbs: 5 gm	Sodium: 228 mg
Component of Fat: 26%	Cholesterol: 7 mg	Calcium: 134 mg

Salads
and
Fresh Greens

CONTENTS

Creamy Cole Slaw

4 cups grated cabbage
$1/_4$ cup cider vinegar
$1/_4$ cup white wine
1 tablespoon sugar
1 cup non-fat plain yogurt
$1/_2$ teaspoon garlic powder
salt and pepper to taste

SERVES 6

Toss grated cabbage with vinegar. In a separate bowl, whisk together remaining ingredients. Pour over cabbage, toss well. Chill before serving.

Serving: 1/6 Recipe	Calories: 45	Protein: 2 gm
Calories from Fat: 1	Total Fat: 0 gm	Dietary Fiber: 1 gm
Saturated Fat: 0 gm	Carbs: 8 gm	Sodium: 50 mg
Component of Fat: 2%	Cholesterol: 0 mg	Calcium: 74 mg

Mixed Bean Salad

3 cups cooked beans:
    navy, lima, soy,
      pinto and/or lentils
$\frac{1}{2}$ cup non-fat plain yogurt
$\frac{1}{3}$ cup non-fat mayonnaise
1 teaspoon celery seed
1 tablespoon grated onion
1 tablespoon sugar
1 teaspoon pepper
1 teaspoon dry mustard
1 teaspoon sage or curry
$\frac{1}{4}$ cup pickle relish

SERVES 6

Drain beans, mix together, cover and chill.

Whip together remaining ingredients. When beans are cold, stir in dressing and chill at least 2 hours before serving.

Serving: 1/6 Recipe
Calories from Fat: 12
Saturated Fat: .5 gm
Component of Fat: 3%

Calories: 365
Total Fat: 1.5 gm
Carbs: 68 gm
Cholesterol: 0 mg

Protein: 23 gm
Dietary Fiber: 20 gm
Sodium: 239 mg
Calcium: 85 mg

Pesto Potato Salad
with Cherry Tomatoes

4 cups cooked and diced
    baby red potatoes
$^1/_4$ cup olive oil
3 tablespoons red wine
    vinegar
1 tablespoon sugar
$^1/_4$ cup fresh sweet basil,
    chopped fine
1 clove minced garlic
1 teaspoon black pepper
$^1/_2$ cup finely chopped
    watercress
2 tablespoons fresh
    chopped parsley
1 pint cherry tomatoes

SERVES 8

Cover and chill diced potatoes in a large bowl.

In a separate bowl, combine olive oil, vinegar and spices. When potatoes are thoroughly chilled, pour on dressing and lightly toss. Add whole cherry tomatoes and gently mix. Chill before serving.

Serving: 1/8 Recipe	Calories: 184	Protein: 3 gm
Calories from Fat: 64	Total Fat: 7 gm	Dietary Fiber: 3 gm
Saturated Fat: 1 gm	Carbs: 29 gm	Sodium: 12 mg
Component of Fat: 33%	Cholesterol: 0 mg	Calcium: 21 mg

The 27,000 acres of the Cape Cod National Seashore feature miles of bicycle and nature trails, warm-water beaches and sandy dunes. Historic Sandwich is the Cape's oldest town, Woods Hole is home to the marine research center, Chatham is famous for its lighthouse, and Provincetown at the tip of the Cape hosts a bustling artists' colony.

Spicy Bean and Tomato Pasta Salad

3 cups cooked and drained
 pinwheels or other
 small pasta
1 lb. young green beans
2 lbs. fresh tomatoes
$^2/_3$ cup non-fat plain
 yogurt
$^1/_4$ cup non-fat mayonnaise
2 teaspoons lime juice
1 teaspoon dry mustard
1 teaspoon garlic powder
1 teaspoon prepared
 horseradish
1 teaspoon marjoram
$^1/_2$ teaspoon cayenne
 pepper
salt and pepper to taste

SERVES 8

Place pasta in a large bowl, cover and chill. Snap off ends of green beans, cut into bite-sized pieces. Blanch in boiling water 4 minutes, drain. Chop tomatoes into bite-sized pieces. Add green beans and tomatoes to pasta.

In a small bowl, whisk together remaining ingredients. When pasta, beans and tomatoes are thoroughly chilled, gently stir in dressing.

Serving: 1/8 Recipe	Calories: 137	Protein: 6 gm
Calories from Fat: 10	Total Fat: 1 gm	Dietary Fiber: 4 gm
Saturated Fat: 0 gm	Carbs: 28 gm	Sodium: 82 mg
Component of Fat: 7%	Cholesterol: 1 mg	Calcium: 77 mg

Polish Beet Salad with Shrimp

6 medium-sized beets
8 oz. cooked, peeled and
    deveined shrimp
$1/2$ cup grated Vidalia, red
    or purple onion

Dressing:
1 cup non-fat sour cream
2 tablespoons herbed
    vinegar
2 tablespoons safflower
    oil
1 teaspoon tarragon
pinch each of dill, sugar,
    salt and pepper

SERVES 4

Wash beets and cut off ends. Place in pot of boiling water and cook until tender, about 30 minutes. Drain. When cool enough to handle, peel and slice beets. In a bowl, combine beets with grated onion. Cut shrimp into $1/2$-inch pieces, add to beets.

In a separate bowl, whisk together dressing ingredients. Mix half of the dressing with beets and shrimp. Cover both bowls, refrigerate at least 2 hours, then mix in remaining dressing. Chill until ready to serve.

Serving: 1/4 Recipe	Calories: 228	Protein: 17 gm
Calories from Fat: 68	Total Fat: 7.5 gm	Dietary Fiber: 2 gm
Saturated Fat: 1 gm	Carbs: 21 gm	Sodium: 264 mg
Component of Fat: 31%	Cholesterol: 111 mg	Calcium: 120 mg

Easy Caesar

*The anchovy garnish can be served on the side
for those who prefer them, and those who don't.*

$^1/_2$ cup non-fat mayonnaise
1 teaspoon Worcestershire
　　sauce
$^1/_4$ teaspoon Dijon mustard
$^1/_4$ teaspoon salt
$^1/_2$ teaspoon pepper
2 cloves garlic, minced
2 tablespoons olive oil
$^1/_4$ cup lemon juice
2 tablespoons fresh grated
　　Parmesan cheese
2 heads romaine lettuce

Garnishes:
1 small can anchovies
herbed croutons

SERVES 6

In a blender combine mayonnaise, Worcestershire, mustard, salt, pepper, garlic, olive oil and lemon juice. Pulse on and off, and scrape down sides, until well blended. Chill in sealed glass jar at least 1 hour.

Wash romaine and tear into pieces. Toss romaine in salad bowl with dressing and Parmesan. Add anchovies and croutons, or serve on the side.

Serving: 1/6 Recipe	Calories: 75	Protein: 2 gm
Calories from Fat: 46	Total Fat: 5 gm	Dietary Fiber: 1 gm
Saturated Fat: 1 gm	Carbs: 6 gm	Sodium: 284 mg
Component of Fat: 61%	Cholesterol: 1 mg	Calcium: 48 mg

Dandelion Greens Salad

Expand your salad bowl! But be sure to wait until the young dandelion greens are up and harvested before fertilizing your lawn.

2 packed cups fresh young
   dandelion leaves
1 head Boston lettuce
2 hard-boiled eggs
$1/_2$ cup croutons

SERVES 4

Wash and dry dandelion leaves and Boston lettuce. Tear greens and place in salad bowl. Chop hard-boiled eggs and toss with greens.

Dressing:
$1/_2$ cup red wine vinegar
$1/_3$ cup crushed raspberries
$1/_2$ tablespoon olive oil
1 tablespoon sugar
1 clove garlic, minced
1 teaspoon basil
1 teaspoon marjoram
salt and pepper to taste

In a glass jar with a tight-fitting lid, combine dressing ingredients and shake well. Pour over salad, toss. Sprinkle croutons on top.

Serving: 1/4 Recipe	Calories: 106	Protein: 5 gm
Calories from Fat: 44	Total Fat: 5 gm	Dietary Fiber: 3 gm
Saturated Fat: 1 gm	Carbs: 11 gm	Sodium: 81 mg
Component of Fat: 40%	Cholesterol: 106 mg	Calcium: 100 mg

Wild greens salads are an interesting alternative to the standard lettuces in the supermarket. Wild greens are often higher in fiber, vitamins and nutrients than most commercial varieties, whose qualities have been developed for longer shelf-life and shipping stamina. Home-grown leaf greens, vegetable greens and herbs make wonderful mixed salads.

Chilled Endive Salad

6 Belgian endives
$^1/_4$ cup (1 oz.) feta cheese
1 Bermuda onion, sliced
    into very thin rings

Dressing:
$^1/_2$ cup non-fat cottage
    cheese
$^1/_2$ cup non-fat sour cream
1 tablespoon lemon juice
1 clove garlic, minced
1 teaspoon white pepper
3 green olives

SERVES 4

Cut off base ends of endives. Cut in half crosswise, then slice lengthwise into strips. Wash well. Divide among salad plates and crumble feta cheese over endive. Cover with the desired amount of Bermuda onion rings.

In blender, process all dressing ingredients until smooth. Spoon dressing over salads.

Serving: 1/4 Recipe	Calories: 132	Protein: 9 gm
Calories from Fat: 39	Total Fat: 4.5 gm	Dietary Fiber: 2 gm
Saturated Fat: 2.5 gm	Carbs: 14 gm	Sodium: 390 mg
Component of Fat: 29%	Cholesterol: 14 mg	Calcium: 171 mg

Fresh Pea Salad

2 cups fresh shelled peas
$^1/_2$ cup finely chopped
    celery
3 tablespoons grated low-
    fat Cheddar cheese

Dressing:
$^1/_2$ cup non-fat plain
    yogurt
$^1/_2$ cup non-fat cottage
    cheese
1 teaspoon dry mustard
1 tablespoon wine vinegar
1 tablespoon grated onion
1 teaspoon sugar
pinch of cayenne
salt and pepper to taste

SERVES 4

Briefly cook peas and celery in boiling water, about 4 minutes. Drain vegetables, transfer to bowl. Cover and chill.

Combine dressing ingredients in blender, process until smooth. Chill.

When peas and celery are cold, toss with grated cheese and dressing. Keep refrigerated until ready to serve.

Serving: 1/4 Recipe	Calories: 129	Protein: 13 gm
Calories from Fat: 20	Total Fat: 2 gm	Dietary Fiber: 5 gm
Saturated Fat: 1.5 gm	Carbs: 16 gm	Sodium: 209 mg
Component of Fat: 15%	Cholesterol: 8 mg	Calcium: 174 mg

Portsmouth Harbor Light,
New Hampshire

Rye Beach Salmon Salad

1 lb. fresh salmon fillet
4 cups water
2 tablespoons vinegar

Sauce:
1/2 cup non-fat
       mayonnaise
1/2 cup non-fat sour cream
2 tablespoons chopped
       scallions
2 tablespoons chili sauce
3 tablespoons fresh
       chopped parsley
1 teaspoon
       Worcestershire sauce
1 tablespoon lemon juice
1 teaspoon basil
pinch of pepper

SERVES 4 (2 AS A MAIN DISH)

Poach salmon fillet in boiling water with vinegar, just until cooked through (a 1/2-inch thick fillet will be poached in 8-10 minutes). Drain fish. When cool enough to handle, peel off skin and cut into bite-sized pieces. Place in covered bowl, refrigerate to chill.

Whip together sauce ingredients. Chill.

When fish and sauce are both cold, lightly fold sauce into salmon. Serve cold.

Serving: 1/4 Recipe	Calories: 188	Protein: 19 gm
Calories from Fat: 49	Total Fat: 5.5 gm	Dietary Fiber: 1 gm
Saturated Fat: 1 gm	Carbs: 13 gm	Sodium: 387 mg
Component of Fat: 28%	Cholesterol: 47 mg	Calcium: 65 mg

The famous yachting race, America's Cup, made its home in Newport, Rhode Island for 50 years. The South County beaches are lined with magnificent mansions belonging to celebrities and important American figures. If you're planning a trip to Newport, why not coordinate it with Newport's Great Chowder Cookoff for a great seafood festival!

Crab Aspic

4 cups tomato juice
2 tablespoons lemon juice
1 teaspoon paprika
1 teaspoon tarragon
1 bay leaf
3 tablespoons chopped
    onion
3 tablespoons finely
    chopped celery leaves
$1/2$ teaspoon celery salt
$1/2$ teaspoon white pepper
pinch of sugar
3 tablespoons gelatin
$1/2$ cup cold vegetable
    bouillon broth
1 lb. fresh crabmeat

SERVES 6

Simmer tomato juice, lemon juice, paprika, tarragon, bay leaf, onion, celery leaves, salt, pepper and sugar 30 minutes. Remove bay leaf.

Soak gelatin in cold broth, then dissolve into the hot juice. Cool at room temperature, then pour into mold and chill. When almost ready to set, sprinkle crabmeat evenly over aspic and fold in. Chill until firm.

To unmold: Briefly set lower part of mold in warm water. Turn onto platter, serve at once.

Serving: 1/8 Recipe   Calories: 107   Protein: 16 gm
Calories from Fat: 10   Total Fat: 1 gm   Dietary Fiber: 0 gm
Saturated Fat: 0 gm   Carbs: 9 gm   Sodium: 364 mg
Component of Fat: 9%   Cholesterol: 57 mg   Calcium: 85 mg

Strawberry-Rhubarb Salad Mold

2 cups finely chopped
  rhubarb
3¹/₂ cups water
2 tablespoons lemon juice
2 pkgs. strawberry-
  flavored gelatin
1 quart fresh strawberries,
  sliced

SERVES 8

Simmer rhubarb in water and lemon juice until tender. Stir in gelatin, mixing until dissolved. Pour into wet mold and chill. When gelatin begins to set, stir in strawberries. Chill until firm, preferably overnight.

Serving: 1/8 Recipe   Calories: 47   Protein: 1 gm
Calories from Fat: 3   Total Fat: .5 gm   Dietary Fiber: 2 gm
Saturated Fat: 0 gm   Carbs: 11 gm   Sodium: 16 mg
Component of Fat: 6%   Cholesterol: 0 mg   Calcium: 38 mg

Poppy Seed Dressing

MAKES 1$\frac{1}{2}$ CUPS

$\frac{1}{4}$ cup honey
1 teaspoon dry mustard
2 teaspoons grated orange
   rind
$\frac{1}{4}$ cup lemon juice
1 tablespoon sugar
$\frac{1}{2}$ cup wine vinegar
$\frac{1}{2}$ cup non-fat plain
   yogurt
2 tablespoons poppy seeds

In blender, combine honey, mustard, orange rind, lemon juice, sugar, vinegar and yogurt, processing until smooth. Transfer into bowl and stir in poppy seeds. Adjust seasonings to taste. Chill at least 4 hours.

Serving: 2 Tablespoons	Calories: 39	Protein: 1 gm
Calories from Fat: 6	Total Fat: .5 gm	Dietary Fiber: 0 gm
Saturated Fat: 0 gm	Carbs: 8 gm	Sodium: 6 mg
Component of Fat: 13%	Cholesterol: 0 mg	Calcium: 35 mg

French Dill Dressing

MAKES 1$\frac{1}{2}$ CUPS

1 tablespoon dill
2 teaspoons marjoram
1 clove garlic, chopped
1 cup tomato purée
$\frac{1}{4}$ cup lemon juice
1 teaspoon mustard
1 tablespoon sugar
$\frac{1}{4}$ cup olive oil
$\frac{1}{4}$ cup vinegar
salt and pepper to taste

Combine all ingredients in blender, process until smooth. Transfer into pot, and simmer 20 minutes. Adjust seasonings to taste. Transfer into jar, chill.

Serving: 2 Tablespoons	Calories: 58	Protein: 1 gm
Calories from Fat: 42	Total Fat: 4.5 gm	Dietary Fiber: 1 gm
Saturated Fat: .5 gm	Carbs: 4 gm	Sodium: 43 mg
Component of Fat: 70%	Cholesterol: 0 mg	Calcium: 22 mg

Creamy Peppercorn Dressing

$^1/_2$ cup softened non-fat
    cream cheese
1 cup non-fat sour cream
1 tablespoon grated
    Parmesan cheese
1 teaspoon garlic powder
$^1/_4$ teaspoon salt
1 tablespoon fresh
    ground peppercorns

MAKES $1^1/_2$ CUPS

Cut softened cream cheese into small pieces. Combine in blender with sour cream, process until smooth. With blender running, add Parmesan and spices. Chill.

Serving: 2 Tablespoons	Calories: 37	Protein: 3 gm
Calories from Fat: 3	Total Fat: .5 gm	Dietary Fiber: 0 gm
Saturated Fat: 0 gm	Carbs: 5 gm	Sodium: 128 mg
Component of Fat: 7%	Cholesterol: 1 mg	Calcium: 53 mg

Herbed Buttermilk Dressing

1 cup non-fat buttermilk
2 tablespoons parsley
1 tablespoon grated onion
1 teaspoon rosemary
1 teaspoon savory
1 clove crushed garlic
1 tablespoon blue cheese
1 cup non-fat mayonnaise

MAKES 2 CUPS

Whip all ingredients in blender. Transfer to bowl and adjust seasonings. Chill.

Serving: 2 Tablespoons	Calories: 19	Protein: 1 gm
Calories from Fat: 3	Total Fat: .5 gm	Dietary Fiber: 0 gm
Saturated Fat: 0 gm	Carbs: 3 gm	Sodium: 129 mg
Component of Fat: 16%	Cholesterol: 1 mg	Calcium: 25 mg

Soups,

Stews

and

Chowders

CONTENTS

Bountiful Bouillabaisse

1½ tablespoons olive oil
4 leeks, white stalks only
6 peeled tomatoes
½ teaspoon fennel
2 teaspoons saffron
2 bay leaves
1 tablespoon finely grated
    orange rind
2 tablespoons tomato paste
1 teaspoon celery seed
3 tablespoons parsley
salt and pepper to taste
2 lbs. very fresh fish cut
    in small pieces
24 mussels, well-scrubbed
24 clams, well-scrubbed
2 cups water
½ cup dry white wine
½ cup fish broth
8 thick slices French bread

SERVES 8

Heat oil in large pot. Wash and slice leek stalks into thin strips and sauté. Chop tomatoes and reserve their juices. Add tomatoes and juices to leeks with fennel, saffron, bay leaves, orange rind, tomato paste, celery seed, parsley, salt and pepper. Simmer 15 minutes on medium-high heat.

Place fish in pot, but do not stir. Layer with mussels and then clams. Pour in water, wine and fish broth. Cover pot and boil 20 minutes.

Place Frech bread slices in 300° oven to toast. Put toasted bread in soup bowls. Arrange fish and shellfish on and around bread, and ladle broth over all.

Serving: 1/8 Recipe	Calories: 350	Protein: 38 gm
Calories from Fat: 68	Total Fat: 7.5 gm	Dietary Fiber: 3 gm
Saturated Fat: 1 gm	Carbs: 30 gm	Sodium: 384 mg
Component of Fat: 20%	Cholesterol: 60 mg	Calcium: 163 mg

Sorrel Soup

1 tablespoon safflower oil
1 cup chopped yellow
    onion
2 cloves garlic, minced
8 packed cups fresh sorrel
    leaves, stems removed
3 cups vegetable bouillon
    broth
3 tablespoons Italian
    parsley
1 teaspoon nutmeg
pinch of white pepper
pinch of dill
pinch of salt
1 cup non-fat sour cream

SERVES 4

Heat oil in pot. Sauté onion and garlic. Wash sorrel leaves and add to pot. Cover and steam 5 minutes. Add bouillon broth, parsley, nutmeg, pepper, dill and salt. Boil, then reduce heat and simmer 45 minutes.

Pour mixture into blender and purée until smooth. Sorrel soup can be served hot or cold. Garnish with sour cream in bowls.

Serving: 1/4 Recipe
Calories from Fat: 51
Saturated Fat: .5 gm
Component of Fat: 23%

Calories: 211
Total Fat: 5.5 gm
Carbs: 32 gm
Cholesterol: 0 mg

Protein: 11 gm
Dietary Fiber: 3 gm
Sodium: 165 mg
Calcium: 96 mg

Classic Ogunquit Onion Soup

SERVES 4

3 large white Spanish
    onions, sliced into
    thin rings
1 clove garlic, minced
$1/2$ tablespoon butter
2 cups white wine
4 cups vegetable bouillon
    broth
4 slices French bread,
    stale or toasted
$1/2$ cup fresh grated
    Parmesan cheese

Sauté onion rings and garlic in butter and wine. Simmer about 1 hour, one cup of liquid remains. Turn down heat.

Preheat broiler. In a separate pot, boil bouillon broth.

Divide cooked onion mixture between 4 ovenproof soup bowls. Ladle hot bouillon broth over the onion. Place a slice of French bread on top, and sprinkle with Parmesan cheese.

Set bowls on a baking sheet and slide under broiler. In 2-3 minutes the cheese will be melted and browned. Serve at once.

Serving: 1/4 Recipe	Calories: 287	Protein: 9 gm
Calories from Fat: 50	Total Fat: 5.5 gm	Dietary Fiber: 4 gm
Saturated Fat: 3 gm	Carbs: 32 gm	Sodium: 406 mg
Component of Fat: 17%	Cholesterol: 12 mg	Calcium: 201 mg

New England Clam Chowder

12 large quahog or
    36 littlenecks
2 cups boiling water
1 medium-sized onion,
    chopped fine
1 teaspoon butter
2 cups peeled and diced
    potatoes
$\frac{1}{4}$ teaspoon salt
1 teaspoon oregano
1 teaspoon basil
1 teaspoon black pepper
3 cups skim milk blended
    with $1\frac{1}{2}$ cups non-fat
    powdered milk

SERVES 4

Scrub clams, discard any that do not close. Steam in boiling water 20 minutes. Strain clam juice through fine sieve, and reserve.

Sauté onion in butter. Add potatoes, spices, milk and 1 cup reserved clam juice. Simmer until potatoes are tender.

Shuck clams and coarsely chop meat. When potatoes are cooked, add clams and cook 10 minutes longer. Adjust seasonings, serve hot.

Serving: 1/4 Recipe	Calories: 304	Protein: 28 gm
Calories from Fat: 23	Total Fat: 2.5 gm	Dietary Fiber: 3 gm
Saturated Fat: 1 gm	Carbs: 42 gm	Sodium: 446 mg
Component of Fat: 7%	Cholesterol: 40 mg	Calcium: 610 mg

Lobster Pot Stew

$^3/_4$ lb. cooked lobster meat
$^1/_2$ lb. crabmeat
$^1/_2$ lb. cleaned squid or
    flounder
2 teaspoons butter
$^1/_3$ cup chopped onion
$^1/_3$ cup chopped celery
1 cup clam juice
4 cups skim milk blended
    with $1^1/_2$ cups non-fat
    powdered milk
1 tablespoon tomato paste
$^1/_4$ teaspoon celery salt
$^1/_4$ teaspoon pepper

SERVES 8

Cut lobster meat into bite-sized pieces. Pick through crab and check for shells. Cut squid or flounder into pieces.

Sauté onion and celery in butter. Add clam juice, milk, tomato paste and spices. Simmer 20 minutes. Add lobster, crab and squid or flounder. Heat 10 minutes, but do not boil.

Serving: 1/8 Recipe	Calories: 206	Protein: 30 gm
Calories from Fat: 23	Total Fat: 2.5 gm	Dietary Fiber: 0 gm
Saturated Fat: 1 gm	Carbs: 14 gm	Sodium: 537 mg
Component of Fat: 12%	Cholesterol: 85 mg	Calcium: 371 mg

The lobster pot, baited with fish scraps, is used to lure and trap lobsters through a netting that they cannot get out of. Lobstermen frequently find crabs, sea urchins, squid, starfish, small fish and even eels that have entered the lobster pot. The pots are checked at least every other day, to remove the legal catch and return others to the sea.

Baked Seafood Chowder

1$^1/_2$ lbs. whitefish (ocean
    cat, haddock, hake)
2 cups diced potatoes
1 cup sliced onion rings
$^1/_2$ cup chopped celery
    leaves
1 clove garlic, minced
1 teaspoon pepper
1 teaspoon basil
$^1/_2$ cup vermouth
2 cups boiling fish
    bouillon broth
1 tablespoon butter
3 cups skim milk blended
    with 1 cup non-fat
    powdered milk

SERVES 6

Preheat oven to 350°. Skin and cut whitefish into bite-sized pieces. In a 4-quart covered casserole, combine all ingredients, except milk. Mix well, cover and bake 1 hour.

Remove casserole and stir in milk. Replace lid and let set 10 minutes before serving.

Serving: 1/6 Recipe
Calories from Fat: 34
Saturated Fat: 2 gm
Component of Fat: 13%

Calories: 273
Total Fat: 3.5 gm
Carbs: 24 gm
Cholesterol: 74 mg

Protein: 32 gm
Dietary Fiber: 2 gm
Sodium: 494 mg
Calcium: 368 mg

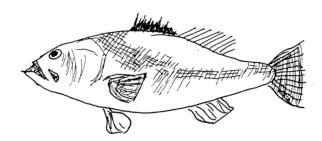

Massachusetts Bay Scallop Chowder

SERVES 4

2 teaspoons butter
2 teaspoons canola oil
$^1/_2$ cup sliced onion rings
1 lb. small bay scallops
1$^1/_2$ cups diced potatoes
3 cups skim milk blended
    with 1 cup non-fat
    powdered milk
3 drops Tabasco sauce
2 tablespoons chopped
    parsley
salt and pepper to taste

Over a medium-high heat, warm butter and oil in a saucepan. Add onion rings and sauté. Pat scallops dry on paper towels, then add to saucepan. Cook scallops until lightly browned, then remove pan from heat.

In a separate pot, simmer potatoes in milk until tender. Add sautéed onions and scallops, Tabasco, parsley, salt and pepper. Heat until thoroughly warmed, but do not boil.

Serving: 1/4 Recipe
Calories from Fat: 52
Saturated Fat: 2 gm
Component of Fat: 16%

Calories: 329
Total Fat: 6 gm
Carbs: 36 gm
Cholesterol: 49 mg

Protein: 33 gm
Dietary Fiber: 2 gm
Sodium: 396 mg
Calcium: 477 mg

Salmon Bisque

$^1/_2$ lb. cooked salmon,
    fresh or canned
$^1/_2$ cup very dry sherry
    (not cooking sherry)
2 teaspoons butter
$^1/_2$ cup very dry red wine
4 tablespoons flour
3 cups skim milk blended
    with 1 cup non-fat
    powdered milk
1 tablespoon
    Worcestershire sauce
salt and pepper to taste

SERVES 4

Using a fork, flake salmon into small pieces, while removing bones and skin. Soak flaked salmon in sherry for 1 hour, then drain.

Heat butter and red wine, blend in flour to make a roux. Whisk in milk, stirring constantly until thick and smooth. Mix in Worcestershire sauce, salt and pepper. Stir in salmon and heat thoroughly, do not boil.

Serving: 1/4 Recipe
Calories from Fat: 55
Saturated Fat: 2 gm
Component of Fat: 19%

Calories: 294
Total Fat: 6 gm
Carbs: 25 gm
Cholesterol: 43 mg

Protein: 25 gm
Dietary Fiber: 0 gm
Sodium: 281 mg
Calcium: 449 mg

Curried Zucchini Bisque

1 cup chopped yellow
    onion
1 tablespoon butter
5 cups chopped zucchini,
    fresh or frozen
2 cups peeled and diced
    potatoes
2 cups vegetable
    bouillon broth
1 cup skim milk blended
    with 1 cup non-fat
    powdered milk
2 teaspoons curry
salt and pepper to taste

SERVES 4

In a large pot, sauté onion in butter. Add zucchini, potatoes and broth. Simmer until potatoes are very soft.

Process cooked mixture in blender or food mill. Return to cooking pot, and simmer 5 minutes. Add milk, curry, salt and pepper.

Serving: 1/4 Recipe	Calories: 219	Protein: 12 gm
Calories from Fat: 34	Total Fat: 4 gm	Dietary Fiber: 4 gm
Saturated Fat: 2 gm	Carbs: 36 gm	Sodium: 189 mg
Component of Fat: 15%	Cholesterol: 12 mg	Calcium: 328 mg

Springtime in New England is heralded by maple sugaring. Amid spring flurries, sugar houses open their doors for demonstrations and tasting. Other signs of spring are flower bulb and daffodil shows, Boston's Reenactment of Paul Revere's Ride, sidewalk art and musical exhibits, sheep shearing and spinning festivals, and antique shows.

Split Pea Porridge

Split Pea Porridge (Soup) can be served right after it is made, but it develops its fullest flavor if warmed up after a day or two in refrigerator.

1 lb. dried split peas
8 cups water
1 cup chopped onion
3 peeled and diced carrots
2 stalks diced celery
2 cloves garlic, minced
2 tablespoons tamari or
    soy sauce
1 teaspoon rosemary
1 small onion stuck with
    6 cloves
2 bay leaves
salt and pepper to taste

Serve with:
croutons

SERVES 6

Rinse split peas in cold water. Combine all ingredients in a large covered pot. Stirring occasionally, simmer about 3 hours, adding water if needed. Remove bay leaves and onion with cloves. Adjust seasonings to taste.

Serve hot with croutons floating on top.

Serving: 1/6 Recipe	Calories: 267	Protein: 18 gm
Calories from Fat: 9	Total Fat: 1 gm	Dietary Fiber: 19 gm
Saturated Fat: 0 gm	Carbs: 49 gm	Sodium: 407 mg
Component of Fat: 3%	Cholesterol: 0 mg	Calcium: 78 mg

Lima Bean Vegetable Stew

If you can make this stew ahead of time,
the aromatic flavors will "marry" and blend.

SERVES 8

1 cup dried baby lima
   beans
4 cups boiling water
2 tablespoons vinegar
$^1/_2$ cup chopped yellow
   onion
1 cup thinly sliced carrot
   rounds
1 cup diced celery
1 cup shredded cabbage
2 cups skim milk
4 tablespoons chopped
   parsley
2 tablespoons
   Worcestershire sauce
$^1/_2$ teaspoon pepper

Soak lima beans in cold water overnight. Drain, rinse, and place in large covered pot of boiling water and vinegar. Simmer 30 minutes and check for tenderness. If needed add more water and cook until beans are tender. Add onion, carrot, celery and cabbage. Simmer another 30 minutes, then reduce heat. Stir in milk, Worcestershire sauce and pepper. Cook 10 more minutes, then adjust seasonings to taste.

Serving: 1/8 Recipe	Calories: 127	Protein: 8 gm
Calories from Fat: 4	Total Fat: .5 gm	Dietary Fiber: 7 gm
Saturated Fat: 0 gm	Carbs: 23 gm	Sodium: 112 mg
Component of Fat: 3%	Cholesterol: 1 mg	Calcium: 124 mg

Cream of Mushroom Soup

5 medium-sized potatoes
2 lbs. whole mushrooms
1 cup chopped onion
2 cups vegetable bouillon
   broth
2 cups skim milk blended
   with 1 cup non-fat
   powdered milk

SERVES 4

Peel and quarter potatoes. Cut mushrooms in half. Place potatoes, mushrooms, onion and broth in covered pot. Simmer until very soft. Process vegetables and cooking water through food mill (or food processor, but texture will be bland). Return to cooking pot and add blended milk, heat to warm but do not boil.

Serving: 1/4 Recipe
Calories from Fat: 14
Saturated Fat: .5 gm
Component of Fat: 4%

Calories: 331
Total Fat: 1.5 gm
Carbs: 65 gm
Cholesterol: 5 mg

Protein: 18 gm
Dietary Fiber: 6 gm
Sodium: 199 mg
Calcium: 393 mg

The Algonquin, Penobscot, Abnaki, Wampanoag and Narragansett Indians were known to the Europeans who settled the New England coast. The Algonquin and Penobscot Indians spent the summer fishing, and digging clams and oysters along the New England coasts and river beds. Some of the catch was then smoked and dried for winter meals.

Asparagus Tip Soup with Watercress

This recipe uses the upper part of the asparagus, but don't throw the rest away! Add the flavor of asparagus to soup stocks or blend into sauces.

4 cups vegetable bouillon
   broth
1 tablespoon herbed
   vinegar
2 cups peeled and diced
   potatoes
$^1/_2$ cup chopped onion
1 clove garlic, minced
1 bay leaf
1 teaspoon thyme
2 cups asparagus, upper
   third of stalk only,
   cut in $^1/_2$-inch pieces
2 packed cups chopped
   watercress
1 cup skim milk
salt and pepper to taste

SERVES 6

In a large pot, boil bouillon broth, vinegar, potatoes, onion, garlic, bay leaf, thyme, until potatoes are very soft. Remove bay leaf. Scoop out potatoes with a slotted spoon, mash, and mix back into hot broth.

Add chopped asparagus to pot, simmer 4 minutes. Stir in watercress, cook 3 minutes then remove pot from heat. Add milk and adjust seasonings to taste.

Serving: 1/6 Recipe	Calories: 98	Protein: 4 gm
Calories from Fat: 2	Total Fat: .5 gm	Dietary Fiber: 2 gm
Saturated Fat: 0 gm	Carbs: 21 gm	Sodium: 112 mg
Component of Fat: 2%	Cholesterol: 1 mg	Calcium: 85 mg

Fisherman's Stew

1¹/₂ lbs. assorted saltwater
    fish: sea bass, cod,
    haddock, cuttlefish,
    flounder, halibut...
¹/₂ cup chopped onion
¹/₂ cup chopped celery
1 cup peeled and diced
    potatoes
1 tablespoon canola oil
1¹/₂ cups chopped peeled
    tomatoes and juice
2¹/₂ cups skim milk
    blended with 1 cup
    non-fat powdered milk
1 tablespoon
    Worcestershire sauce
¹/₄ teaspoon salt
1 teaspoon pepper

SERVES 6

Wash and cut fish into bite-sized pieces. In a large pot, sauté onion, celery and potatoes in oil for 10 minutes. Add chopped tomatoes and their juice, cover pot and simmer until potatoes are tender. Stir in fish and simmer 15 minutes.

Remove pot from heat and add milks, Worcestershire sauce, salt and pepper. Warm on low heat, but do not boil.

Serving: 1/6 Recipe	Calories: 233	Protein: 30 gm
Calories from Fat: 33	Total Fat: 3.5 gm	Dietary Fiber: 1 gm
Saturated Fat: .5 gm	Carbs: 20 gm	Sodium: 328 mg
Component of Fat: 14%	Cholesterol: 69 mg	Calcium: 319 mg

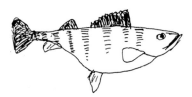

Main
Meal
Dishes

CONTENTS

Any fish, cooked by any means, generally requires only 10 minutes of cooking time for each inch of thickness, measured at its thickest part.

Pastry Fish Pie

SERVES 6

Pastry Dough:

$2^1/_2$ cups all-purpose flour
$2^1/_2$ tablespoons canola oil
1 egg beaten with
    1 egg white
4 tablespoons ice water
$^1/_2$ cup skim milk

Pie Filling:

2 teaspoons canola oil
$^1/_2$ cup chopped onion
$^1/_2$ cup chopped celery
$1^1/_2$ cups peeled and diced
    potatoes or rutabaga
$1^1/_4$ cups skim milk
$1^1/_2$ lbs. bluefish or tuna
    chunks
2 tablespoons
    Worcestershire sauce
2 teaspoons black pepper
$1^1/_2$ cups peas

In a large bowl, cut oil and beaten eggs into flour with pastry cutter or knives until evenly distributed. With a fork, blend in ice water, then $^1/_2$ cup skim milk.

Spray a 9" pie pan with non-stick oil. Place two-thirds of the dough in pan. Press with oiled fingers to $^1/_4$-inch thick on bottom and sides. Bake 10 minutes in 350° oven.

Sauté onion and celery in 2 teaspoons of oil. Add potatoes or rutabaga, milk and spices. Cook until soft, then coarsely mash together. Poach fish in water for 10 minutes. Combine fish with mashed vegetables, Worcestershire, pepper and peas. Pour into pie crust. Place spoonfuls of remaining dough on top of pie, and flatten with oiled fingers to cover top. Bake in 350° oven 30 minutes. Cool 5 minutes before cutting.

Serving: 1/6 Recipe	Calories: 490	Protein: 39 gm
Calories from Fat: 91	Total Fat: 10 gm	Dietary Fiber: 5 gm
Saturated Fat: 1.5 gm	Carbs: 59 gm	Sodium: 163 mg
Component of Fat: 19%	Cholesterol: 88 mg	Calcium: 152 mg

Steamed Lobster and Clams in Spring Herbs

3 cups water
1 cup sorrel leaves
2 tablespoons lemon balm
6 medium potatoes
6 dozen steamer clams
6 lobsters, 1-1½ lbs. each

Serve with:
2 tablespoons hot butter
melted with 1 tablespoon
lemon juice and 1 cup of
white wine

SERVES 6

Boil water and herbs in a covered 24-quart steamer to a rolling boil. Put potatoes in pot 20 minutes before adding lobsters.

Scrub clams, discarding any with broken shells or that do not close tightly when handled. Tie clams by the dozen, in squares of cheesecloth tied with string. Allow room in bags for clams to open.

Place lobsters in steaming pot. Cover. After 15 minutes, add steamer bags. Cover and steam until clams open, about 15 minutes. In a saucepan, combine ingredients for hot butter, then serve in dipping bowl.

Serving: 1/6 Recipe	Calories: 434	Protein: 50 gm
Calories from Fat: 65	Total Fat: 7.5 gm	Dietary Fiber: 3 gm
Saturated Fat: 3 gm	Carbs: 34 gm	Sodium: 553 mg
Component of Fat: 15%	Cholesterol: 197 mg	Calcium: 164 mg

How to Eat
Lobster and Clams

Lobster: Bend back claws and flippers, break off where attached to body. Use cracker and pick out meat in claws and knuckles. Suck meat from flippers.

Bend back tail and break off from body. Tail flippers can also be broken back and the meat pushed out, or you can cut the membrane. In the body are the green tomalley (liver) and the red coral of the females (roe).

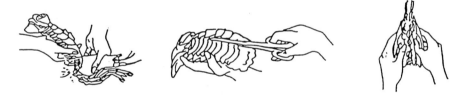

Clams: Wedge open shells and loosen meat. Dip in broth to rinse off sand.

Scalloped Oysters

The oysters and mixtures can be prepared in advance, but do not combine in casserole until just before baking.

3 cups shucked raw oysters
and their liquor
(reserved from
shucking oysters)
2 cups plain bread toast
or cracker crumbs
3 tablespoons grated
Parmesan cheese
pinch of cayenne
1 tablespoon canola oil
$^1/_2$ cup skim milk blended
with $^1/_4$ cup non-fat
powdered milk
$^1/_2$ teaspoon nutmeg
$^1/_2$ teaspoon ground celery
seeds
$^1/_2$ teaspoon pepper

SERVES 4

Preheat oven to 350°. Spray a deep-dish casserole with 3 coats non-stick oil. Prepare oysters and their liquor.

Combine crumbs with grated Parmesan cheese and cayenne. Drizzle oil over crumbs and blend with fork. In a separate bowl, combine milks and spices.

Dust casserole with 3 tablespoons of the crumb mixture. then layer with half of the oysters and their liquor, and half of the milk mixture. Cover with $1^1/_4$ cups crumbs. Complete with layers of remaining oysters, milk and crumbs. Bake 20 minutes, then briefly set under hot broiler to brown on top.

Serving: 1/4 Recipe	Calories: 264	Protein: 19 gm
Calories from Fat: 94	Total Fat: 10.5 gm	Dietary Fiber: 1 gm
Saturated Fat: 2.5 gm	Carbs: 23 gm	Sodium: 434 mg
Component of Fat: 36%	Cholesterol: 106 mg	Calcium: 263 mg

Tarragon Shrimp Tempura

If the oil is very hot flavors will be quickly sealed in, tempura will be crispy, and less oil absorbed.

2 lbs. large raw shrimp,
    peeled and deveined
3 tablespoons unbleached
    flour
2 tablespoons cornstarch
2 teaspoons tarragon
pinch of salt
$^1/_2$ teaspoon pepper
$^1/_2$ cup water
$^3/_4$ cup canola oil
lemon wedges and/or
prepared seafood sauce

SERVES 6

Rinse shrimp and pat dry on towels.

In a mixing bowl, combine flour, cornstarch, tarragon, salt and pepper. Blend in water, cover, and chill 20 minutes.

Preheat oven to 300°. Line a baking sheet with paper towels. Heat oil in a small, deep pan to 350°-375°.

Dip shrimp in batter, allowing excess to drip off. Fry in hot oil until golden brown, about 1 minute on each side. Place fried shrimp on lined baking sheet in oven. Serve with lemon wedges or prepared sauce.

Serving: 1/6 Recipe	Calories: 266	Protein: 31 gm
Calories from Fat: 108	Total Fat: 12 gm	Dietary Fiber: 0 gm
Saturated Fat: 1 gm	Carbs: 7 gm	Sodium: 244 mg
Component of Fat: 41%	Cholesterol: 230 mg	Calcium: 93 mg

Mystic Scallops in Vermouth Sauce

$1^1/_2$ lbs. sea scallops, cut
    in quarters
2 cups sliced mushrooms
2 cloves garlic, minced
2 teaspoons butter
1 tablespoon olive oil
3 tablespoons flour
1 cup skim milk
$^1/_2$ cup dry vermouth
pinch of cayenne
salt and white pepper to
    taste

SERVES 4

In a large pan, sauté scallops, mushrooms and garlic in hot butter and olive oil. When scallops have begun to brown and mushrooms are tender, remove them with a slotted spoon and arrange in a baking dish.

Blend flour into hot liquid in pan. Over medium heat, whisk in milk and stir until thick and smooth. Reduce heat and add vermouth, cayenne, salt and pepper. When sauce has thickened, spread over scallops and mushrooms. Briefly place under broiler until golden brown.

Serving: 1/4 Recipe	Calories: 265	Protein: 32 gm
Calories from Fat: 63	Total Fat: 7 gm	Dietary Fiber: 1 gm
Saturated Fat: 2 gm	Carbs: 13 gm	Sodium: 357 mg
Component of Fat: 24%	Cholesterol: 63 mg	Calcium: 124 mg

In the 1700's, poorer New England families drank hard cider at every meal. Wealthier households used hard cider to supplement other liquors, but it was still consumed in great volume. In 1721, at a small village near Boston consisting of about 40 families, 3,000 barrels of "Cyder" (about 95,000 gallons) was produced and quaffed in that year alone!

Lemon Trout

4 fillets of trout, sized to
    suit appetites
salt and pepper to taste
12 round lemon slices
    with seeds removed
1 medium onion, thinly
    sliced in rounds

SERVES 4

Preheat oven to 400° or prepare outdoor grill and allow fire to burn down to hot coals.

Make a "packet" for each serving of trout: fold a double thickness of tin-foil into a 12-inch square. Place trout in middle of foil and sprinkle with salt and pepper. Place 3 lemon slices on each trout and cover with onion rounds. Fold in ends of foil and crease. Bring sides of foil together over fish, fold edges together, and crease into a $1/2$-inch seam. Continue folding and creasing until flat against fish. Place fish packet in oven or on grill. Cook packet 4 minutes on each side.

Serving: 1 Fillet
Calories from Fat: 52
Saturated Fat: 1 gm
Component of Fat: 34%

Calories: 147
Total Fat: 6 gm
Carbs: 6 gm
Cholesterol: 49 mg

Protein: 18 gm
Dietary Fiber: 2 gm
Sodium: 75 mg
Calcium: 61 mg

Grilled Lobster Tails
à la Martha's Vineyard

8 fresh, uncooked lobster
    tails, about 2 lbs.
2 tablespoons lime juice
2 tablespoons white wine
2 tablespoons canola oil
1 teaspoon white pepper
1 teaspoon paprika

Garnish:
lemon wedges

SERVES 4

With a scissors, remove the soft under-cover membrane of lobster tails. Turn tails over and slightly crack back of shell so tails lie flat. Run a skewer through tails to keep them from curling while cooking.

Make a marinade of remaining ingredients. Place lobster tails in marinade, cover and refrigerate until ready to grill.

Prepare grill or preheat broiler. Place skewered lobster tails 4 inches from coals or broiler. Basting frequently, cook 5 minutes on each side. Serve with lemon wedges.

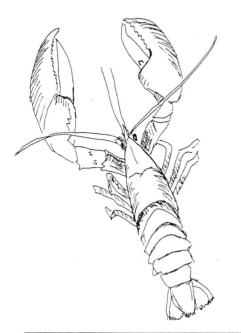

Serving: 2 Lobster Tails	Calories: 241	Protein: 43 gm
Calories from Fat: 51	Total Fat: 5.5 gm	Dietary Fiber: 0 gm
Saturated Fat: .5 gm	Carbs: 2 gm	Sodium: 672 mg
Component of Fat: 22%	Cholesterol: 215 mg	Calcium: 115 mg

Crab Cakes with Green Sauce

1 lb. cleaned crabmeat
$^1/_2$ cup diced red pepper
1 tablespoon white wine
$^1/_3$ cup non-fat
    mayonnaise
1 teaspoon Dijon mustard
2 teaspoons
    Worcestershire sauce
1 egg, beaten
$^1/_4$ cup bread crumbs
salt and pepper to taste
2 tablespoons canola oil

Green Sauce:
$^3/_4$ cup canned green chili
    peppers, drained and
    chopped
3 tablespoons vinegar
2 teaspoons sugar

SERVES 4

Clean crabmeat. Pat dry in a paper towel.

Simmer red pepper in wine. In a mixing bowl, combine pepper with remaining ingredients, except canola oil. Let set 15 minutes, then form into 3-inch cakes. Spray large skillet with non-stick oil. Coat with canola oil. Fry crab cakes on each side until nicely browned.

Green Sauce: In a small saucepan, simmer all ingredients 20 minutes. Serve in a small demi-cup on the side of crab cakes.

Serving: 1/4 Recipe	Calories: 250	Protein: 26 gm
Calories from Fat: 95	Total Fat: 10.5 gm	Dietary Fiber: 1 gm
Saturated Fat: 1 gm	Carbs: 12 gm	Sodium: 519 mg
Component of Fat: 38%	Cholesterol: 166 mg	Calcium: 145 mg

Poached Flounder Mornay

1½ lbs. flounder fillets
1 tablespoon canola oil
2 tablespoons flour
1 cup skim milk
½ teaspoon celery salt
1 tablespoon dry sherry
pinch of ground cloves
pinch of cayenne
salt and pepper to taste
1 tablespoon grated
   shallots
1 egg yolk, beaten
3 tablespoons grated
   Parmesan cheese
3 tablespoons non-fat
   sour cream

SERVES 4

Poach flounder in simmering water while preparing mornay. Poach just until springy.

Heat oil in saucepan, blend in flour, whisk skim milk into flour stirring until thick and smooth. Stir in celery salt, sherry, cloves, cayenne, salt, pepper and grated shallots. Continue cooking and stirring for 2 minutes.

Remove from heat and blend in beaten egg yolk. Return to heat and whisk 4 minutes. Remove from heat. Stir in grated cheese and sour cream. Spoon mornay over flounder fillets and brown lightly under broiler.

Serving: 1 Recipe	Calories: 568	Protein: 32 gm
Calories from Fat: 75	Total Fat: 8.5 gm	Dietary Fiber: 8 gm
Saturated Fat: 1 gm	Carbs: 92 gm	Sodium: 328 mg
Component of Fat: 13%	Cholesterol: 49 mg	Calcium: 89 mg

Real Thing Fish & Chips

*These fabulous English fish & chips are a popular treat at Maine fairs,
if you don't mind waiting in a 30 minute line for great food.*

fresh cod or haddock fillets
ocean water or flat beer
unpeeled potatoes sliced
    into $^3/_8$-inch thick
    sticks
unbleached white flour
canola oil
malt vinegar
2 pinches sea salt
newspaper

PREPARE $^1/_4$ LB. FISH AND
2 POTATOES PER PERSON

Cut cod or haddock into serving-sized pieces. Soak fish in actual ocean water (not salted water) or use flat beer. Prepare potatoes.

In a deep frying pan, heat $1^1/_2$-inches of canola oil to 370°-375°. Dip fish in flour, back into ocean water, and into the flour, again. Fry with potatoes until golden brown (the flour holds in the fish's juice and flavor.) Drain on paper towels. Sprinkle lightly with malt vinegar and sea salt. Fold each serving of fish and chips in newspaper, leaving an opening at the top.

Serving: 1 Recipe	Calories: 568	Protein: 32 gm
Calories from Fat: 75	Total Fat: 8.5 gm	Dietary Fiber: 8 gm
Saturated Fat: 1 gm	Carbs: 92 gm	Sodium: 328 mg
Component of Fat: 13%	Cholesterol: 49 mg	Calcium: 89 mg

John Nute, a/k/a "Real Thing Fish & Chips," lives on the Blue Hill Peninsula. He travels to the Blue Hill Fair and the Scottish Festival in Brunswick to serve up authentic English fish & chips in his mobile fry-shop, a double-decker bus brought from England. John says "nothing refreshes the taste of fish like sea water, but in a pinch, beer will do."

Creamed Connecticut Codfish

2 lb. box salt codfish
1 tablespoon butter
1 tablespoon safflower oil
4 tablespoons flour
2 cups skim milk
1 egg, beaten
1 teaspoon Worcestershire
   sauce
1 teaspoon pepper
pinch of nutmeg
6 slices toast

SERVES 6

Soak codfish in cold water 4-6 hours, changing water every hour to remove salt. Place fish in a medium sauce pan, and cover with fresh water. Cook over medium heat for 15 minutes. Drain.

In a separate saucepan, heat butter and oil. Blend in flour . Remove saucepan from heat and whisk in milk, then beaten egg. Return to stove and cook until thickened. Stir in Worcestershire sauce, pepper and nutmeg. Gently fold in fish and heat briefly. Serve Creamed Codfish over toast.

Serving: 1/6 Recipe	Calories: 360	Protein: 49 gm
Calories from Fat: 69	Total Fat: 7.5 gm	Dietary Fiber: 1 gm
Saturated Fat: 2 gm	Carbs: 20 gm	Sodium: 227 mg
Component of Fat: 20%	Cholesterol: 42 mg	Calcium: 142 mg

In the mid-eighteenth century, Europeans who fished the banks of New England's coast returned home with fabulous tales of the abundance of cod. As the mainstay of the colonists' diet, Cape Cod was justly named. Scrod refers to cod weighing 2 pounds or under. Salt cod can be tough, and may be pounded out between desalting soakings in fresh water.

Salmon Mousse
with Chilled Cucumber Sauce

2 tablespoons unflavored
    gelatin
$^1/_4$ cup cold water
$^1/_2$ cup boiling water
$^1/_2$ cup non-fat
    mayonnaise
1 tablespoon lemon juice
1 tablespoon grated onion
1 teaspoon paprika
1 lb. poached salmon
2 cups non-fat cottage
    cheese
1 cup non-fat sour cream
1 medium sized cucumber
1 teaspoon dill
2 teaspoons prepared
    mustard
salt and pepper to taste

SERVES 6

Soften gelatin in cold water. Add boiling water, stir until dissolved. Rest 10 minutes, then stir in mayonnaise, lemon juice, onion and paprika. Chill until it begins to thicken.

Use a fork to flake salmon into tiny pieces. Remove gelatin mixture from refrigerator and fold in salmon, cottage cheese and $^1/_3$ cup of the sour cream. Pour into fish mold and chill.

Peel, seed and dice cucumber. Combine in blender with sour cream and spices. Process until smooth. Chill. Serve cold cucumber sauce spooned over unmolded salmon mousse.

Serving: 1/6 Recipe	Calories: 241	Protein: 31 gm
Calories from Fat: 45	Total Fat: 5 gm	Dietary Fiber: 1 gm
Saturated Fat: 1 gm	Carbs: 15 gm	Sodium: 499 mg
Component of Fat: 19%	Cholesterol: 42 mg	Calcium: 113 mg

Poached salmon is vintage New England cooking. Use fresh herbs, wine and herbed vinegars in the poaching liquid to add the essence of these flavors. Delicate fishes can be wrapped in cheesecloth before poaching. A classic spring meal includes chowder, new peas, baked bread, potatoes and a fresh strawberry pie.

Salmon Soufflé

2 teaspoons flour
2 cups skim milk blended
　　with $^1/_2$ cup non-fat
　　powdered milk
2 tablespoons butter
$^1/_2$ cup flour
2 eggs, separated
2 egg whites
2 teaspoons
　　Worcestershire sauce
pinch of dry mustard
salt and pepper to taste
2 lbs. fresh poached
　　salmon

SERVES 6

Preheat oven to 375°. Spray 2-quart soufflé with non-stick oil, dust with 2 teaspoons flour.

Put milk in small pot to boil. Melt butter in another saucepan, then blend in $^1/_2$ cup flour. Quickly pour boiling milk into flour mixture, whisk until thick and smooth. Cool at room temperature.

Beat in egg yolks, Worcestershire sauce, mustard, salt and pepper. Flake salmon apart with a fork, then fold into mixture.

With an electric beater, beat egg whites until stiff. Lightly fold into salmon mixture. Pour into prepared soufflé. Bake 35-40 minutes, or until golden brown on top. Serve at once.

Serving: 1/6 Recipe
Calories from Fat: 101
Saturated Fat: 4 gm
Component of Fat: 32%

Calories: 323
Total Fat: 11 gm
Carbs: 13 gm
Cholesterol: 163 mg

Protein: 40 gm
Dietary Fiber: 0 gm
Sodium: 287 mg
Calcium: 238 mg

Grilled Swordfish Amandine

4 teaspoons sliced almonds
4 fresh swordfish steaks,
    about 1¹/₂ lbs.
1 teaspoon melted butter
1 teaspoon lemon juice

SERVES 4

Toast almond slices on cookie sheet in oven until lightly browned.

Prepare outdoor grill, or preheat indoor grilling surface. Before placing grill over flames, spray with non-stick oil. Place swordfish on grill and lightly brush with butter and lemon juice. When brown, flip over and lightly brush second side with butter and lemon juice. When inner flesh is opaque, serve hot off the grill. Sprinkle 1 teaspoon almond slices on each piece.

Serving: 1 Steak	Calories: 232	Protein: 34 gm
Calories from Fat: 83	Total Fat: 9 gm	Dietary Fiber: 0 gm
Saturated Fat: 2.5 gm	Carbs: 1 gm	Sodium: 163 mg
Component of Fat: 37%	Cholesterol: 69 mg	Calcium: 14 mg

In 1860, the New England colonies distilled over 4,000,000 gallons of rum from molasses. Maine produced 452,000 gallons, although in 1851 it had enacted the first dry law in the nation (all rum was presumably exported.) But with hundreds of Maine islands to hide behind, rum-runners did a good trade, explaining the states' numerous "Rum Islands."

Seafood and Pea Curry

1$^1/_2$ tablespoons safflower
  oil
3 tablespoons flour
1 cup fish broth
1 cup white wine
1 teaspoon lemon juice
$^1/_2$ teaspoon dry mustard
1 teaspoon nutmeg
1 tablespoon curry powder
$^3/_4$ cup skimmed
  evaporated milk
2 cups cooked lobster meat
  and/or other seafood
1 cup fresh shelled peas,
  lightly steamed
3 cups cooked rice

SERVES 4

Heat oil in a saucepan. Blend in flour, then broth, wine, lemon juice, mustard, nutmeg and curry powder. Stir constantly until thickened. Remove from heat, mix in evaporated milk.

Fold lobster and/or seafood, and steamed peas into curry sauce. Warm on low heat. Serve curry in bowls with rice.

Serving: 1/4 Recipe   Calories: 443   Protein: 33 gm
Calories from Fat: 66   Total Fat: 7.5 gm   Dietary Fiber: 3 gm
Saturated Fat: 1 gm   Carbs: 50 gm   Sodium: 447 mg
Component of Fat: 15%   Cholesterol: 63 mg   Calcium: 237 mg

Mystic, Connecticut

Pasta, Beans

and Grains

CONTENTS

Any Pasta, Beans and Grains recipe can be used for a
main dish or side dish by varying the amount per person.

Shells with White Clam Sauce

2 tablespoons chopped
  shallots
2 teaspoons minced garlic
2 tablespoons olive oil
3 tablespoons chopped
  parsley
pinch of red pepper flakes
2 teaspoons all-purpose
  flour
1 cup white wine
$^2/_3$ cup clam juice
$1^1/_2$ cups canned or fresh
  steamed clams, rinsed
  and minced
1 teaspoon butter
3 tablespoons Parmesan
  cheese
8 oz. dry medium shells

SERVES 4

Sauté shallots and garlic in olive oil. Add parsley and red pepper flakes. Whisk in flour, then white wine and clam juice. Simmer until liquid is reduced by half.

Stir in clams. Remove from heat, mix in butter and Parmesan cheese. Cover pan and place on very low heat.

Boil pasta shells until tender. Drain well. Divide among dinner plates and spoon white clam sauce on top.

Serving: 1/4 Recipe	Calories: 348	Protein: 9 gm
Calories from Fat: 90	Total Fat: 10 gm	Dietary Fiber: 1 gm
Saturated Fat: 2.5 gm	Carbs: 45 gm	Sodium: 383 mg
Component of Fat: 26%	Cholesterol: 8 mg	Calcium: 76 mg

Pawtucket Crab and Pasta

2 cups small dry pasta
1 teaspoon safflower oil
1 tablespoon safflower oil
$^1/_2$ cup chopped onion
1 cup chopped celery
1 cup sliced mushrooms
$^1/_4$ cup dry sherry
1 teaspoon pepper
1 teaspoon tarragon
1 cup low-fat sour cream
2 tablespoons non-fat
    mayonnaise
1 lb. fresh crabmeat
2 tablespoons breadcrumbs
1 teaspoon paprika

SERVES 4

Boil pasta until tender, but firm to the bite. Drain well, toss with 1 teaspoon oil.

Sauté onion and celery in 1 tablespoon oil. When lightly browned, add mushrooms, dry sherry, pepper and tarragon. Simmer together for 5 minutes. Remove from heat and stir in sour cream and mayonnaise. Set aside some nice pieces of crab leg meat, and lightly fold in the rest. Gently mix in pasta.

Preheat oven to 350°. Spray a casserole with non-stick oil. Transfer mixture to casserole. Arrange crab leg meat on top of casserole, then sprinkle with breadcrumbs and paprika. Bake 20 minutes. Serve at once.

Serving: 1/4 Recipe	Calories: 459	Protein: 33 gm
Calories from Fat: 63	Total Fat: 7 gm	Dietary Fiber: 3 gm
Saturated Fat: 1 gm	Carbs: 61 gm	Sodium: 474 mg
Component of Fat: 14%	Cholesterol: 89 mg	Calcium: 218 mg

Shepherd's Pie

SERVES 6

2¹/₂ cups mashed potatoes
¹/₂ teaspoon salt
2 tablespoons chopped
    walnut crumbs
¹/₂ cup all-purpose flour
1¹/₂ tablespoons canola oil
2 eggs, lightly beaten
1 tablespoon canola oil
¹/₂ cup chopped onion
¹/₂ cup chopped celery
2 cloves garlic, minced
1¹/₂ cups diced potatoes
1 cup peeled and diced
    rutabaga
1 cup diced carrots
1¹/₂ cups skim milk
2 teaspoons black pepper
2 tablespoons
    Worcestershire sauce
1 cup peas
1 cup chopped asparagus

Combine mashed potatoes, salt, walnut crumbs, flour, oil and eggs to make potato dough. Spray a 9" x 12" baking pan with non-stick oil. Using ²/₃ of the dough, place spoonfuls of dough in pan and press with oiled fingers to ¹/₄-inch thickness on bottom and sides of pan. Bake 10 minutes in 350° oven.

Sauté onion, celery and garlic in oil. Add potatoes, rutabaga, carrots, milk, pepper and Worcestershire. Cook until potatoes are soft. Partially mash potatoes, rutabagas and carrots. Mix in remaining ingredients, cook 5 minutes more. Pour into baking pan. Place spoonfuls of remaining dough on top of vegetables, and flatten with oiled fingers until covered. Bake in preheated 350° oven 30 minutes. Cool 5 minutes before cutting.

Serving: 1/6 Recipe	Calories: 283	Protein: 10 gm
Calories from Fat: 86	Total Fat: 9.5 gm	Dietary Fiber: 6 gm
Saturated Fat: 1 gm	Carbs: 41 gm	Sodium: 333 mg
Component of Fat: 30%	Cholesterol: 72 mg	Calcium: 144 mg

Eggplant and Pasta Parmesan

3 medium-sized eggplants
3 tablespoons olive oil
2 cups dry small elbow
    macaroni
2 cups prepared tomato
    sauce seasoned with
    oregano, garlic, basil
pinch of salt
pinch of pepper
$^1/_2$ cup grated part-skim
    mozzarella cheese
$^1/_4$ cup grated Parmesan
    cheese

SERVES 6

Peel eggplants and slice them vertically into $^1/_2$-inch thick pieces. Spray a large frying pan with non-stick oil and cover with a coat of olive oil. Heat oil and brown eggplant on both sides. Repeat until all eggplant is fried.

Boil macaroni in a full pot of water until tender, but firm to the bite. Drain. Return macaroni to pot and stir in tomato sauce.

Spray baking dish with non-stick oil. Arrange two layers each of macaroni, eggplant and mozzarella. Cover with Parmesan. Bake in a 350° oven 25 minutes, or until bubbly.

Serving: 1/6 Recipe	Calories: 264	Protein: 10 gm
Calories from Fat: 86	Total Fat: 9.5 gm	Dietary Fiber: 4 gm
Saturated Fat: 2.5 gm	Carbs: 37 gm	Sodium: 327 mg
Component of Fat: 32%	Cholesterol: 8 mg	Calcium: 147 mg

Vegetables Amandine with Noodles

2 cups dry small noodles
3 tablespoons blanched
    almond slivers
1 tablespoon safflower oil
2 tablespoons white wine
$1/2$ teaspoon poppy seeds
1 clove minced garlic
1 tablespoon lemon juice
pinch of cayenne
pinch of saffron
$1/4$ teaspoon salt
$1/4$ teaspoon pepper
3 cups mixed fresh
    vegetables, steamed
    and drained

SERVES 6

Boil noodles in water until tender. Drain. Toast almonds on cookie sheet until browned.

In a large skillet heat oil, add almonds, wine, poppy seeds, garlic, lemon juice and spices. Stir in steamed vegetables and heat until warmed, then gently toss in cooked noodles.

Serving: 1/6 Recipe
Calories from Fat: 50
Saturated Fat: .5 gm
Component of Fat: 23%

Calories: 216
Total Fat: 5.5 gm
Carbs: 35 gm
Cholesterol: 0 mg

Protein: 7 gm
Dietary Fiber: 3 gm
Sodium: 123 mg
Calcium: 52 mg

Seafood Curried Rice

2 cups water
2 cups beer
1 cup white or brown rice
$^1/_2$ cup wild rice
1 teaspoon butter
1 cup peeled and chopped
    tomatoes
$^1/_2$ cup chopped onion
$^1/_2$ cup chopped green
    pepper
2 cloves minced garlic
$^1/_2$ teaspoon black pepper
pinch of salt
2 teaspoons curry powder
2 cups raw bay scallops or
    small peeled shrimp

SERVES 4

Bring water and beer to a full boil. Remove from heat, add rice and butter. Cover and rest 45 minutes, then mix in remaining ingredients. Spray casserole with non-stick oil, transfer rice into casserole.

Preheat oven to 350°. Bake about $1^1/_2$ hours, stirring occasionally. Curried rice is done when liquid is absorbed, but rice is still moist.

Serving: 1/4 Recipe	Calories: 390	Protein: 20 gm
Calories from Fat: 33	Total Fat: 3.5 gm	Dietary Fiber: 4 gm
Saturated Fat: 1 gm	Carbs: 65 gm	Sodium: 165 mg
Component of Fat: 8%	Cholesterol: 25 mg	Calcium: 56 mg

Rice is an aquatic grass and grows in moist climates throughout the world. It is a traditional food of many diverse cultures. The wild rice of North America is abundant in lakes and ponds of the north central states. Its introduction to New England is believed to have been made by migratory ducks, and wild rice now flourishes here as well.

Risotto with Asparagus

1 medium onion, diced
1 tablespoon olive oil
$1/4$ cup chopped celery
1 clove garlic, minced
2 cups dry arborio rice
$1/2$ cup dry sherry
1 tablespoon powdered
    vegetable stock or
    crushed bouillon cube
6 cups boiling water
1 lb. fresh asparagus, cut
    into $1/2$-inch pieces
2 peeled tomatoes,
    chopped and drained
1 tablespoon butter
$1/2$ teaspoon black pepper
$1/4$ cup fresh grated
    Parmesan cheese

SERVES 8 (4 AS A MAIN DISH)

In a large saucepan, sauté onion in oil. Add celery and garlic. When onion is clear, stir in rice, turn heat to high and add sherry. Turn heat to medium when liquid is reduced by half.

In a separate pot, mix powdered stock or bouillon into 6 cups boiling water. Remove from heat and add asparagus to broth. Blanch asparagus, then strain from broth.

Pour broth into risotto, $1/2$ cup at a time. Stir, and allow rice to absorb liquid after each addition. After final addition of broth, some liquid will remain. Stir in blanched asparagus and chopped tomatoes, cook 5 minutes more adding liquid if needed. When rice is soft and creamy, stir in butter, pepper and Parmesan.

Serving: 1/8 Recipe	Calories: 290	Protein: 7 gm
Calories from Fat: 38	Total Fat: 4 gm	Dietary Fiber: 3 gm
Saturated Fat: 2 gm	Carbs: 52 gm	Sodium: 201 mg
Component of Fat: 14%	Cholesterol: 6 mg	Calcium: 80 mg

Leek Pilaf

SERVES 6

3 leeks
1 tablespoon olive oil
1 cup regular bulgur
   (not fine ground)
2 cups vegetable bouillon
   broth
$\frac{1}{2}$ cup carrot, diced
$\frac{1}{4}$ cup celery, diced
$\frac{1}{2}$ cup red pepper, diced
2 scallions, diced
1 teaspoon marjoram
2 tablespoons parsley
2 tablespoons finely
   chopped pecans

Remove outer leaves from leeks, reserving only the white fleshy stalk and the lower tender parts of the green leaves. Wash thoroughly and slice into rounds.

Heat oil in large saucepan. Add leeks and sauté 3 minutes, then mix in bulgur. Stir in broth, carrot, celery, pepper, scallions and marjoram. Cover pan, simmer 40 minutes, or until bulgur is tender. Mix in parsley.

Toast chopped pecans on cookie sheet in oven. Toss pecans into pilaf, and serve hot.

Serving: 1/6 Recipe	Calories: 177	Protein: 5 gm
Calories from Fat: 39	Total Fat: 4.5 gm	Dietary Fiber: 7 gm
Saturated Fat: .5 gm	Carbs: 32 gm	Sodium: 58 mg
Component of Fat: 21%	Cholesterol: 0 mg	Calcium: 58 mg

Portsmouth, New Hampshire was founded as a fishing village in 1624. Its earliest settlement, Strawberry Banke, has been restored as a marvelous architectural display of colonial America. In 1905, President Roosevelt brought the Russians and Japanese to the Portsmouth Naval Shipyard to sign the treaty that ended the Russo-Japanese War.

Steamed Millet

1 cup millet
2¹/₂ cups water
¹/₄ teaspoon salt

Serve with vegetables or substitute for pasta or rice

SERVES 4

Wash millet. Boil in salted water 30 minutes, or until tender.

Millet is a flavorful light grain, and makes an excellent side dish to almost any meal.

Serving: 1/4 Recipe	Calories: 189	Protein: 6 gm
Calories from Fat: 19	Total Fat: 2 gm	Dietary Fiber: 4 gm
Saturated Fat: .5 gm	Carbs: 37 gm	Sodium: 152 mg
Component of Fat: 10%	Cholesterol: 0 mg	Calcium: 7 mg

House of the Pearl
Orrs Island, Portland, Maine

Boston Baked Beans

3 cups dried navy beans
1 gallon water
4 tablespoons molasses
4 tablespoons brown
   sugar
2 tablespoons dry mustard
1 can beer
$\frac{1}{4}$ teaspoon salt
$\frac{1}{4}$ teaspoon pepper

SERVES 8

Wash beans. Boil in 1 gallon water for 5 minutes. Remove from heat and let set 1 hour. Return to stove and boil 1 hour. Drain beans, then transfer to bean pot. Stir in remaining ingredients, and cover.

Bake in 250° oven for 6 hours, adding water as needed. Uncover pot and bake 25 minutes more, while beans brown on top.

Serving: 1/8 Recipe
Calories from Fat: 9
Saturated Fat: .5 gm
Component of Fat: 3%

Calories: 330
Total Fat: 1 gm
Carbs: 63 gm
Cholesterol: 0 mg

Protein: 18 gm
Dietary Fiber: 21 gm
Sodium: 95 mg
Calcium: 219 mg

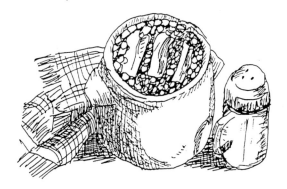

Roasted Chestnut and Bean Casserole

1 lb. small white beans
6 cups vegetable bouillon
   broth
1 lb. chestnuts in shells
2 tablespoons canola oil
2 onions, chopped
2 eggs
1 cup skim milk
3 tablespoons Parmesan
   cheese

SERVES 8

Wash beans, soak overnight, rinse, and drain. Boil beans in vegetable broth, adding water if needed. When tender, drain and mash.

Score an "X" into bottom of chestnuts. Place on cookie sheet in 350° oven. Roast 20-30 minutes. When cool, crack open and chop chestnut meats into small pieces.

Sauté onions in oil. In a small bowl, beat eggs, milk and cheese. Combine beans, chestnuts, onion and milk mixture. Transfer into a casserole that's been sprayed with non-stick oil. Bake in 350° oven 30 minutes.

Serving: 1/8 Recipe	Calories: 408	Protein: 19 gm
Calories from Fat: 60	Total Fat: 6.5 gm	Dietary Fiber: 15 gm
Saturated Fat: 1.5 gm	Carbs: 70 gm	Sodium: 138 mg
Component of Fat: 14%	Cholesterol: 55 mg	Calcium: 187 mg

Lima Beans in Sautéed Garlic

1 lb. dried baby lima
    beans
2 tablespoons safflower
    oil
2 shallots
6-8 cloves garlic, minced
3 tablespoons vermouth
1 teaspoon ground cloves
$1/2$ teaspoon salt
$1/2$ teaspoon black pepper
1 teaspoon savory
1 teaspoon sage
2 tablespoons fresh
    parsley

SERVES 6

Wash lima beans and soak overnight. In the morning, drain, and put beans in a large pot of boiling water. Cover and simmer until tender, about 1 hour. Do not allow beans to overcook and become mushy.

Just before beans are finished cooking, heat oil in saucepan. Slice shallots into crescent-shaped pieces. Sauté shallots and garlic in oil. Mix in vermouth and spices, reduce heat.

Drain lima beans, and stir into saucepan with garlic sauce. Serve at once.

Serving: 1/6 Recipe	Calories: 310	Protein: 16 gm
Calories from Fat: 48	Total Fat: 5.5 gm	Dietary Fiber: 16 gm
Saturated Fat: .5 gm	Carbs: 50 gm	Sodium: 206 mg
Component of Fat: 15%	Cholesterol: 0 mg	Calcium: 81 mg

The use of garlic in America came from the recipes of the European immigrants. Although long prevalent in American homes with strong cultural traditions, garlic was not popular until the 1960's, when diverse ethnic cooking styles became fashionable. Today, garlic is commonly used in many American recipes.

Vegetables

and

Sauces

CONTENTS

Cinnamon Glazed Carrots

3 lbs. carrots
2$^1/_2$ cups water
1 tablespoon cider vinegar
$^1/_2$ cup honey
$^1/_2$ cup maple syrup
2 teaspoons cinnamon
1 teaspoon nutmeg
pinch of salt

SERVES 6

Peel carrots and cut into sticks. Boil water in a large saucepan, add carrots and cover. Boil 5 minutes, or until carrots are tender. Drain.

Bring vinegar, honey, syrup and spices to a boil. Reduce heat and simmer, uncovered, 10 minutes or until thickened. Pour over carrots. Serve hot.

Serving: 1/6 Recipe   Calories: 256   Protein: 2 gm
Calories from Fat: 7   Total Fat: 1 gm   Dietary Fiber: 7 gm
Saturated Fat: 0 gm   Carbs: 63 gm   Sodium: 143 mg
Component of Fat: 3%   Cholesterol: 0 mg   Calcium: 41 mg

Corn Pudding

2 cups mashed corn
   kernels
2 eggs, slightly beaten
1$\frac{1}{2}$ cups skim milk
1$\frac{1}{2}$ tablespoons safflower
   oil
1 tablespoon honey
salt and pepper to taste

SERVES 6

Preheat oven to 350°. Spray a 1-quart casserole, or six individual custard cups with non-stick oil.

Mash corn kernels before measuring. Mix in remaining ingredients. Pour into prepared casserole or dishes. Place casserole or custard cups in large oven pan filled with $\frac{1}{2}$-inch water.

Bake casserole 50 minutes or custard cups 40 minutes. Cool 5 minutes before serving.

Serving: 1/6 Recipe	Calories: 131	Protein: 6 gm
Calories from Fat: 47	Total Fat: 5 gm	Dietary Fiber: 1 gm
Saturated Fat: 1 gm	Carbs: 17 gm	Sodium: 75 mg
Component of Fat: 33%	Cholesterol: 72 mg	Calcium: 85 mg

Fresh Steamed Peas

**fresh shelled peas or
fresh snow pea pods**

PREPARE $\frac{1}{2}$-CUP PEAS PER PERSON

Briefly wash peas in cold water. If using snow pea pods, snap off stem end.

Boil water in covered pot. Place peas in boiling water, cook just until tender (about 10 minutes for shelled peas, and 5 minutes for snow pea pods). Sweet, fresh spring peas are absolutely perfect as they are, but you may want to try steaming them in light broth, or add wine, lemon juice or a little butter to the boiling water. A few grains of salt are often preferred, but not necessary.

Serving: 1/2 Cup	Calories: 59	Protein: 4 gm
Calories from Fat: 3	Total Fat: .5 gm	Dietary Fiber: 4 gm
Saturated Fat: 0 gm	Carbs: 11 gm	Sodium: 4 mg
Component of Fat: 4%	Cholesterol: 0 mg	Calcium: 18 mg

Herbed Green Beans

1 lb. fresh green beans
1 tablespoon olive oil
3 tablespoons chopped
    scallions
$\frac{1}{3}$ cup finely chopped
    celery
2 cloves crushed garlic
$\frac{1}{2}$ teaspoon basil
$\frac{1}{2}$ teaspoon rosemary
$\frac{1}{2}$ teaspoon thyme
$\frac{1}{2}$ teaspoon pepper
1 tablespoon chopped
    parsley
$\frac{1}{4}$ teaspoon salt
$\frac{1}{4}$ teaspoon pepper

SERVES 5

Parboil green beans about 6 minutes, drain.

In a saucepan over medium-low heat, sauté scallions, celery and garlic in oil until celery is tender. Add green beans and remaining spices. Cover and cook 5 minutes longer. Toss and serve immediately.

Serving: 1/5 Recipe	Calories: 62	Protein: 2 gm
Calories from Fat: 27	Total Fat: 3 gm	Dietary Fiber: 3 gm
Saturated Fat: .5 gm	Carbs: 9 gm	Sodium: 127 mg
Component of Fat: 39%	Cholesterol: 0 mg	Calcium: 59 mg

Prior to the discovery of America, the Europeans only knew of "broad-beans" and the Oriental soybean. The Indians of the Americas had been cultivating Lima beans, scarlet runners, string beans and many varieties of shell beans for centuries. Since beans are easy to grow and early to mature, many kinds were planted extensively by the colonists.

Basted Oven Tomatoes

This recipe has much less fat than it appears,
as most of the oil is left behind in the pan.

SERVES 6

6 large beefsteak-type or
    9 medium tomatoes
3 tablespoons fresh, finely
    chopped parsley
2 large cloves crushed
    garlic
$\frac{1}{4}$ teaspoon salt
$\frac{1}{2}$ teaspoon black pepper
6 tablespoons olive oil

Preheat oven to 325°. Wash tomatoes in cold water and slice in half across the width.

Select a stove-top/baking pan in which the tomato halves can be tightly placed, side-by-side. Spray pan with non-stick oil. Arrange tomatoes cut side up in pan. Cover with parsley, garlic, salt and pepper. Pour olive oil over tomatoes. Place on stovetop burner over medium-high heat 15 minutes. Spoon liquids in pan over tomatoes. Bake 1 hour in oven, occasionally basting with liquid in pan. Tomatoes will be black and half their original size. Remove with slotted spatula, allowing cooking oil to drain back into pan.

Serving: 1/6 Recipe
Calories from Fat: 46
Saturated Fat: .5 gm
Component of Fat: 51%

Calories: 81
Total Fat: 5 gm
Carbs: 9 gm
Cholesterol: 0 mg

Protein: 2 gm
Dietary Fiber: 2 gm
Sodium: 115 mg
Calcium: 14 mg

Mushroom Velvet

2 tablespoons green onion
   slivers
1 tablespoon safflower oil
1 lb. sliced mushrooms

Velouté Sauce:
1 tablespoon safflower oil
1 tablespoon flour
1 cup vegetable broth
3 tablespoons white wine
$1/4$ teaspoon nutmeg
$1/4$ teaspoon salt
$1/4$ teaspoon pepper

SERVES 4

Prepare green onion slivers by discarding the tough ends of the green leaves, and using only the white fleshy parts and the lower tender green leaves in the inner layers. Slice into thin slivers. Heat safflower oil in saucepan. Sauté green onion in hot oil for 2 minutes, reduce heat, and add mushrooms. Cook until mushrooms are just tender.

To prepare Velouté (Velvet) Sauce: Heat oil in a small saucepan. Blend in flour, then whisk in broth and wine. Beat until smooth, add spices and cook until thickened. Mix into mushrooms.

Serving: 1/4 Recipe	Calories: 115	Protein: 3 gm
Calories from Fat: 66	Total Fat: 7.5 gm	Dietary Fiber: 2 gm
Saturated Fat: .5 gm	Carbs: 9 gm	Sodium: 175 mg
Component of Fat: 54%	Cholesterol: 0 mg	Calcium: 10 mg

Garlic Broccoli

1 head of broccoli
1¹/₂ tablespoons olive oil
1 teaspoon lemon juice
¹/₄ cup white wine
¹/₄ teaspoon salt
¹/₄ teaspoon pepper
3-4 cloves garlic

SERVES 4

Divide broccoli into large florets. Place on vegetable steamer over boiling water. Cover pot and steam 10 minutes, or until broccoli has just turned tender and dark green.

In a small saucepan, heat olive oil, lemon juice, wine, salt and pepper. Cut garlic cloves into quarters, add to saucepan and sauté over medium-low heat for 10 minutes.

Place broccoli in serving bowl. Strain garlic sauce over broccoli.

Serving: 1/4 Recipe	Calories: 92	Protein: 4 gm
Calories from Fat: 50	Total Fat: 5.5 gm	Dietary Fiber: 4 gm
Saturated Fat: 1 gm	Carbs: 8 gm	Sodium: 182 mg
Component of Fat: 48%	Cholesterol: 0 mg	Calcium: 70 mg

Parsleyed Cauliflower

1 medium cauliflower
1 tablespoon butter
1 teaspoon olive oil
1 tablespoon lemon juice
2 pinches salt
$\frac{1}{4}$ teaspoon white pepper
3 tablespoons fresh
    chopped parsley

SERVES 4

Separate cauliflower florets into sections. Wash in cold water. Steam on vegetable steamer just until tender. Place in serving bowl.

Melt butter with olive olive, lemon juice and seasonings. Pour over hot cauliflower.

Serving: 1/4 Recipe	Calories: 76	Protein: 5 gm
Calories from Fat: 42	Total Fat: 4.5 gm	Dietary Fiber: 6 gm
Saturated Fat: 2 gm	Carbs: 7 gm	Sodium: 163 mg
Component of Fat: 48%	Cholesterol: 8 mg	Calcium: 52 mg

Scalloped Potatoes

3 tablespoons flour
$^1/_2$ teaspoon salt
$^1/_4$ teaspoon black pepper
6 medium-sized potatoes,
    peeled and cut in
    thin half-rounds
3 tablespoons grated
    onion
$^1/_3$ cup grated low-fat
    cheddar cheese
2 cups skim milk
1 tablespoon safflower oil

SERVES 6

Preheat oven to 375°. Combine flour, salt and pepper. Spray a $1^1/_2$-quart casserole with non-stick oil. Arrange a layer of half of the potatoes, cover with half of the grated onion, half of the flour and grated cheese. Repeat for second layering of potatoes, onion, flour and cheese. Pour on milk, then oil. Bake about 45 minutes, or until potatoes are tender and browned on top.

Serving: 1/6 Recipe	Calories: 215	Protein: 11 gm
Calories from Fat: 37	Total Fat: 4 gm	Dietary Fiber: 3 gm
Saturated Fat: 1 gm	Carbs: 35 gm	Sodium: 283 mg
Component of Fat: 17%	Cholesterol: 6 mg	Calcium: 263 mg

Sweet Potato Casserole

SERVES 8

3 cups cooked mashed
    sweet potatoes
4 tablespoons honey
1 egg, beaten
1 teaspoon vanilla
$1/3$ cup evaporated skim
    milk
$1/4$ teaspoon salt

Topping:
$1/2$ cup brown sugar
$1/4$ cup flour
$1/4$ cup chopped nuts
1 tablespoon safflower oil

Preheat oven to 350°. Spray a $2^1/2$-quart casserole with non-stick oil. Beat together filling ingredients, and pour into casserole.

Mix topping ingredients together and sprinkle over potato mixture. Bake 30-40 minutes, until lightly golden on top.

Serving: 1/8 Recipe   Calories: 287   Protein: 5 gm
Calories from Fat: 45   Total Fat: 5 gm   Dietary Fiber: 3 gm
Saturated Fat: .5 gm   Carbs: 57 gm   Sodium: 119 mg
Component of Fat: 15%   Cholesterol: 27 mg   Calcium: 84 mg

Fiddleheads

If harvesting fiddlehead ferns from the wild, take only a small proportion from large groupings. Cut in spring when shoots are curled in crosiers.

**fresh cut fiddlehead ferns
washed and tied in
bundles of 6-8 fronds**

2 BUNDLES OF FERNS PER PERSON

Place ferns on vegetable steamer over boiling water. Cover pot and steam 10 minutes or until tender. Serve with lemon juice, salt and pepper, or try the Light Mornay Sauce below.

Serving: 2 Bundles	Calories: 41	Protein: 4 gm
Calories from Fat: 2	Total Fat: 0 gm	Dietary Fiber: 4 gm
Saturated Fat: 0 gm	Carbs: 6 gm	Sodium: 100 mg
Component of Fat: 5%	Cholesterol: 0 mg	Calcium: 28 mg

Light Mornay Sauce

**2 tablespoons canola oil
2 tablespoons flour
$^1/_2$ cup vegetable broth
$^1/_2$ cup skim milk
$^1/_3$ cup grated low-fat
     Swiss Lorraine cheese
1 tablespoon dry sherry
$^1/_4$ teaspoon salt
$^1/_4$ teaspoon white pepper**

SERVES 8

Heat oil in saucepan, blend in flour to make a roux. Slowly whisk in vegetable broth and milk. Cook until thickened. Stir cheese and sherry into sauce. Adjust seasonings to taste, adding salt and pepper if desired.

Serving: 2 Tablespoons	Calories: 55	Protein: 2 gm
Calories from Fat: 34	Total Fat: 4 gm	Dietary Fiber: 0 gm
Saturated Fat: .5 gm	Carbs: 3 gm	Sodium: 98 mg
Component of Fat: 60%	Cholesterol: 2 mg	Calcium: 65 mg

Steamed Spring Greens

1 tablespoon olive oil
3 tablespoons cider vinegar
1 tablespoon honey
1 teaspoon pepper
1 tablespoon chopped
    parsley
2 tablespoons minced
    shallots
$^1/_2$ cup sliced mushrooms
4 cups chopped mixed
    spring greens: young
    dandelion leaves,
    sorrel, watercress

SERVES 4

In a large saucepan, combine all ingredients except chopped mixed greens. Simmer 3 minutes. Measure greens after they have been chopped and packed into the measuring cup. Add greens, cover pan, and stir occasionally. Simmer briefly to desired tenderness.

Serving: 1/4 Recipe	Calories: 76	Protein: 2 gm
Calories from Fat: 34	Total Fat: 4 gm	Dietary Fiber: 2 gm
Saturated Fat: .5 gm	Carbs: 11 gm	Sodium: 43 mg
Component of Fat: 40%	Cholesterol: 0 mg	Calcium: 108 mg

Sautéed Summer Squash

1 clove garlic, minced
1 tablespoon olive oil
1 medium onion, sliced
12 fresh mushrooms,
      sliced to show shape
$^1/_2$ teaspoon rosemary
pinch of cardamom
$^1/_2$ teaspoon pepper
5 cups julienned squash
      and zucchini, sliced
      thinly on a slant
$^1/_3$ cup non-fat plain
      yogurt or sour cream
$^1/_4$ teaspoon salt

SERVES 6

In a large saucepan, sauté garlic in olive oil on medium-low heat until yellow. Add onion and mushrooms, sauté 5 minutes more. Stir in spices and squash, and cook another 5 minutes. Reduce heat to low, cover pan, and simmer 8 minutes.

Mix in yogurt or sour cream and salt. Cover, and turn off heat. Let stand 4 minutes, then serve while still warm.

Serving: 1/6 Recipe	Calories: 58	Protein: 3 gm
Calories from Fat: 23	Total Fat: 2.5 gm	Dietary Fiber: 2 gm
Saturated Fat: .5 gm	Carbs: 8 gm	Sodium: 109 mg
Component of Fat: 35%	Cholesterol: 0 mg	Calcium: 42 mg

Fresh Steamed Asparagus

Asparagus covered with Hollandaise Sauce is a perfect flavor combination.

SERVES 6

2 lbs. fresh asparagus

Cut off bottom ends of asparagus. If stalks are thick, scrape skin off lower end. Set on steamer over boiling water, cover and steam just until tender, about 5-10 minutes.

Serving: 1/6 Recipe	Calories: 35	Protein: 4 gm
Calories from Fat: 8	Total Fat: 1 gm	Dietary Fiber: 2 gm
Saturated Fat: 0 gm	Carbs: 3 gm	Sodium: 20 mg
Component of Fat: 23%	Cholesterol: 0 mg	Calcium: 18 mg

Hollandaise Sauce

SERVES 6

1 tablespoon cornstarch
$^1/_2$ cup water
2 tablespoons lemon juice
pinch of cayenne pepper
$^1/_4$ teaspoon salt
1 egg yolk, beaten
$1^1/_2$ tablespoons butter

Boil water in bottom of a double boiler. In the top pan of double boiler, whisk cornstarch with $^3/_4$-cup cold water. Add lemon juice and spices. Stirring constantly, cook until thick. Whisk in yolks and butter. Stir and cook until thickened into rich sauce.

Serving: 2 Tablespoons	Calories: 43	Protein: 1 gm
Calories from Fat: 35	Total Fat: 4 gm	Dietary Fiber: 0 gm
Saturated Fat: 2 gm	Carbs: 2 gm	Sodium: 130 mg
Component of Fat: 79%	Cholesterol: 44 mg	Calcium: 6 mg

Oven-Baked Parsnips

8 large parsnips
4 cups vegetable bouillon
$1^1/_2$ tablespoons canola oil
1 tablespoon chopped
    parsley

SERVES 6

Wash parsnips, but do not peel. Parboil in bouillon for 10 minutes. Drain, peel off skins, and slice in half lengthwise. If parsnips have a tough inner core, remove and discard. Cut into strips, about 4 inches long and $^1/_2$-inch wide.

Preheat oven to 350°. Place parsnips on baking dish that has been sprayed with non-stick oil. Brush with canola oil. Bake about 30 minutes, or until golden-brown on the outside, and tender inside. Sprinkle with chopped parsley.

Serving: 1/6 Recipe	Calories: 166	Protein: 2 gm
Calories from Fat: 35	Total Fat: 4 gm	Dietary Fiber: 6 gm
Saturated Fat: .5 gm	Carbs: 32 gm	Sodium: 69 mg
Component of Fat: 20%	Cholesterol: 0 mg	Calcium: 55 mg

The New England coastline is quite varied, but beaches can be found in each oceanfront state. Massachusetts, Connecticut and Rhode Island have many miles of beautiful sandy beaches. New Hampshire has the Hampton and Rye Beaches, and there are 36 miles of sandy shore in Maine. In July and August, even Maine's waters can be warm enough for a swim.

Golden Onion Kuchen

4 large onions
1¹/₂ tablespoons butter
1 recipe Buttermilk Biscuit
    (page 22)
1 egg
8-oz. non-fat sour cream
pinch of garlic powder
pinch of salt
¹/₂ teaspoon black pepper
1 teaspoon poppy seeds

SERVES 9

Peel onions and slice into medium-thin rings. Heat butter in a sauté pan. Add onions and sauté until they just begin to clear.

Spray 9-inch square baking pan with non-stick oil. Press biscuit dough into bottom of pan. Cover with sautéed onions.

In a small bowl, beat egg with sour cream, garlic powder, salt and pepper. Spoon on top of onions. Sprinkle poppy seeds over kuchen. Bake 30 minutes in 350° oven. Slice into 9 large pieces. Best if served while still warm.

Serving: 1 Piece	Calories: 206	Protein: 17 gm
Calories from Fat: 55	Total Fat: 6 gm	Dietary Fiber: 2 gm
Saturated Fat: 2.5 gm	Carbs: 33 gm	Sodium: 374 mg
Component of Fat: 21%	Cholesterol: 29 mg	Calcium: 146 mg

Desserts

and

Sweets

CONTENTS

Note: The nutritional analysis for pies is based on 8 pieces per pie.

Fresh Raspberry Cobbler

3 pints clean raspberries
$^1/_2$ cup + 3 tablespoons
　　sugar
1 tablespoon quick
　　tapioca
1 tablespoon fresh lemon
　　juice
2 cups all-purpose flour
pinch of salt
1 tablespoon baking
　　powder
2 tablespoons canola oil
2 tablespoons butter
1 egg
$^1/_2$ cup skim milk

SERVES 8

Preheat oven to 400°. Spray a large casserole or baking dish with non-stick oil.

In a mixing bowl combine raspberries, $^1/_2$-cup sugar, tapioca and lemon juice. Spread into baking dish and let sit 30 minutes.

Combine flour, salt, baking powder, oil, butter and 1 tablespoon sugar with a pastry cutter or fingertips until mixture resembles small peas. In a separate bowl, beat together egg and milk, then stir into flour mixture. Knead lightly in bowl. Break off pieces of dough and gently press over raspberries to form a "cobbled" topping. Sprinkle with remaining 2 tablespoons sugar. Bake 35-40 minutes or until golden brown. Serve warm.

Serving: 1/8 Recipe	Calories: 293	Protein: 5 gm
Calories from Fat: 72	Total Fat: 8 gm	Dietary Fiber: 7 gm
Saturated Fat: 2.5 gm	Carbs: 52 gm	Sodium: 212 mg
Component of Fat: 24%	Cholesterol: 35 mg	Calcium: 111 mg

Apple Strudel

Filling:
8 apples, peeled and cored
2 tablespoons lemon juice
$1^1/_2$ cups golden raisins
$^3/_4$ cup finely chopped
      walnuts or almonds
1 cup sugar
$1^1/_2$ tablespoons quick
      tapioca
1 tablespoon cinnamon

Pastry Dough:
2 cups flour
$^1/_8$ teaspoon baking soda
2 tablespoons sugar
2 eggs
$^1/_4$ cup canola oil
$^1/_2$ teaspoon vinegar
$1^1/_2$ tablespoons warm
      water

Tops: canola oil, sugar
      and cinnamon

Chop apples into very small pieces, place in mixing bowl, sprinkle with lemon juice and toss. Add remaining filling ingredients, mix, cover, and refrigerate at least 8 hours.

Combine pastry dough ingredients in a mixer, and then cover to prevent drying out. On a floured cloth, roll a 2-inch ball of dough into a thin 12" x 8" rectangle. Lightly brush with oil. Place $1^1/_2$-inch wide by $^3/_4$-inch high strip of filling along a 12-inch edge. Use the cloth to raise the edge and roll up strudel. Pinch end and tuck under, and transfer to cookie sheet sprayed with non-stick oil. Place rolls 2 inches apart on sheet. Brush strudels with oil, sprinkle with cinnamon and sugar. Starting $^1/_2$-inch from ends, use a sharp knife to pierce top of rolls. Bake at 350° for 25 minutes. Cool 10 minutes in pan, then place on brown paper. Cut pieces apart at pierced marks.

Serving: 2 Pieces	Calories: 91	Protein: 1 gm
Calories from Fat: 28	Total Fat: 3 gm	Dietary Fiber: 1 gm
Saturated Fat: .5 gm	Carbs: 16 gm	Sodium: 6 mg
Component of Fat: 28%	Cholesterol: 8 mg	Calcium: 9 mg

Strawberry Rhubarb Pie

Filling:
2 full cups strawberries,
   hulled and halved
2 cups chopped rhubarb
$1/_4$ cup flour
$1^1/_2$ cups sugar
2 teaspoons finely grated
   orange rind
pinch of salt
1 tablespoon butter
1 tablespoon sugar (to
   sprinkle over top)

Pie Shell:
$2^2/_3$ cups all-purpose flour
4 tablespoons sugar
pinch of salt
$1/_4$ cup canola oil
$1/_2$ cup cold skim milk

NOTE: Let pie cool an
hour or more before cutting.

MAKES ONE 9-INCH PIE

Combine strawberries, rhubarb, flour, sugar, rind and salt. Let set 15 minutes.

Sift flour, sugar and salt together. In a separate bowl, combine oil and milk. Pour liquid into flour, blend with fork. If too dry to hold together, add a little milk. Wrap in plastic, chill 15 minutes. Divide dough into 2 parts. Between sheets of wax paper, roll one piece of dough round and one rectangular. Place round piece in 9-inch pie pan sprayed with non-stick oil. Cut rectangular dough into $1/_2$-inch strips.

Stir strawberries, then pour into pie shell. Dot top with butter. On 2 perpendicular sides of pie shell, pinch strips of dough to shell and weave into lattice. Trim excess, flute edges and sprinkle with a tablespoon sugar. Bake at 450° 10 minutes. Reduce heat to 350°, bake 30 minutes more.

Serving: 1 Piece	Calories: 426	Protein: 5 gm
Calories from Fat: 82	Total Fat: 9 gm	Dietary Fiber: 3 gm
Saturated Fat: 1.5 gm	Carbs: 82 gm	Sodium: 55 mg
Component of Fat: 19%	Cholesterol: 4 mg	Calcium: 64 mg

Cherry Pie

2²/₃ cups all-purpose flour
4 tablespoons sugar
pinch of salt
¹/₄ cup canola oil
¹/₂ cup cold skim milk
4 cups chopped cherries,
    pitted and halved
2 teaspoons lemon juice
1 cup sugar
¹/₂ teaspoon vanilla extract
1¹/₂ tablespoons cornstarch
¹/₃ cup apple juice
1 tablespoon butter
1 tablespoon sugar

NOTE: Cherry Pie is best after it has cooled and set at least 30 minutes. Try it with non-fat vanilla frozen yogurt on top!

MAKES ONE 9-INCH PIE

Preheat oven to 400°. Spray 9-inch pie pan with non-stick oil.

Sift flour, sugar and salt. In a separate bowl, combine oil and milk. Pour into flour, then blend with fork. If too dry to hold together, add a little milk. Wrap in plastic and chill 15 minutes. Divide dough in half and roll each into a round between two sheets of wax paper. Place one round of dough in pie pan.

Mix cherries, lemon juice, sugar and vanilla. Dissolve cornstarch in apple juice, then stir into cherries. Let rest 15 minutes, then stir again. Pour cherries into crust, spread evenly, and dot with butter. Place top dough round on pie, pinch edges together, flute and trim. Make 5 slits in top crust. Sprinkle with 1 tablespoon sugar. Bake about 35 minutes on upper rack of oven.

Serving: 1 Piece	Calories: 398	Protein: 5 gm
Calories from Fat: 82	Total Fat: 9 gm	Dietary Fiber: 2 gm
Saturated Fat: 1.5 gm	Carbs: 76 gm	Sodium: 42 mg
Component of Fat: 20%	Cholesterol: 4 mg	Calcium: 44 mg

Chocolate-Pecan Ricotta Pie

SERVES 12

Crust:
1 cup low-fat graham
    cracker crumbs
1 tablespoon sugar
1 tablespoon butter
1 egg, beaten

Filling:
$1\frac{1}{2}$ teaspoons unflavored
    gelatin
1 cup skim milk
$\frac{1}{2}$ cup cold reduced-fat
    chocolate chips
$\frac{1}{3}$ cup chopped pecans
15 oz. part-skim Ricotta
    cheese
$\frac{3}{4}$ cup sugar
1 teaspoon vanilla

Optional Topping:
mini-chocolate chips and
    pecans

Combine graham cracker crumbs and sugar in small mixing bowl. Melt butter, then cool slightly. Mix butter and egg into the crumbs. Press into the bottom and sides of 9-inch pie plate. Bake at 350° for 10 minutes. Cool.

In mixing bowl, sprinkle gelatin over $\frac{1}{4}$ cup of milk. Heat, don't boil, the remaining $\frac{3}{4}$ cup milk. Add hot milk to gelatin mixture. Stir well. Chill until consistency is like yogurt.

Place chocolate chips and pecans in blender and whirl 2 minutes. Add ricotta, sugar and vanilla into blender, whip until completely smooth. (Turn off blender and scrape down sides as needed.) Pour into large mixing bowl. Beat gelatin mixture with electric beater until fluffy, then fold into ricotta blend. Pour into pie crust. If desired, decorate top with chips and pecans. Chill 3 hours before serving.

Serving: 1/12 Pie	Calories: 193	Protein: 6 gm
Calories from Fat: 78	Total Fat: 8.5 gm	Dietary Fiber: 0 gm
Saturated Fat: 5 gm	Carbs: 25 gm	Sodium: 82 mg
Component of Fat: 38%	Cholesterol: 32 mg	Calcium: 132 mg

Peaches Flambé

2 tablespoons butter
3 tablespoons brown
   sugar
4 fresh peaches, peeled
2 bananas
3 oz. brandy or dark rum
1 tablespoon sugar

Optional: Non-fat vanilla
   frozen yogurt

SERVES 4

Melt butter over low heat, stir in brown sugar until dissolved. Turn heat to low. Slice peaches into crescent-shaped pieces. Add peaches to butter mixture. Cover pan, but occasionally stir and baste. When peaches start to juice-up, turn heat up to medium-low. Slice bananas lengthwise into quarters, then into 2-inch strips. When peaches are almost tender, add bananas, cook 2 minutes more. Turn off heat and cover.

In a separate saucepan, heat liquor over low heat 4 minutes. Place fruit in casserole or flambé dish, sprinkle with sugar and pour warm liquor over all. Cover for 1 minute. Remove cover, dim lights, stand back, and light! Serve flambé when flame goes out, preferably over frozen yogurt.

Serving: 1/4 Recipe	Calories: 222	Protein: 1 gm
Calories from Fat: 58	Total Fat: 6.5 gm	Dietary Fiber: 3 gm
Saturated Fat: 4 gm	Carbs: 36 gm	Sodium: 67 mg
Component of Fat: 25%	Cholesterol: 16 mg	Calcium: 18 mg

Lemon Meringue Pie

Pie Crust:
1³/₄ cups flour
¹/₂ teaspoon salt
3 tablespoons vegetable
   shortening
3 tablespoons canola oil
6 tablespoons cold water

Pie Filling:
2 small lemons
1 cup sugar
4 tablespoons flour
pinch of salt
3 egg yolks, beaten
2 cups boiling water

Merinque:
3 egg whites
6 tablespoons sugar
¹/₂ teaspoon vanilla
   extract

MAKES ONE 9-INCH PIE

Crust: Mix flour and salt. Cut vegetable shortening and oil into flour with pastry cutter or two knives, until texture resembles peas. Sprinkle with water then blend with fork or fingers. Roll crust between sheets of wax paper. Place in pie plate, trim and flute edges. Bake in 450° oven 12 minutes.

Filling: Boil water in bottom pan of double boiler. Into the top pan, add 2 teaspoons finely grated lemon rind, and the juice of both lemons. Mix in dry ingredients of pie filling, then the beaten egg yolks. While stirring, add boiling water. Cook until thick and clear. Pour into prepared pie shell. Chill.

Meringue: Beat egg whites until stiff. Gradually add sugar and vanilla. Spoon on top of pie filling. Bake at 325° 15 minutes. Chill well before serving.

Serving: 1 Piece	Calories: 405	Protein: 5 gm
Calories from Fat: 108	Total Fat: 12 gm	Dietary Fiber: 1 gm
Saturated Fat: 2.5 gm	Carbs: 70 gm	Sodium: 187 mg
Component of Fat: 26%	Cholesterol: 80 mg	Calcium: 17 mg

Raspberry-Rhubarb Sorbet

Select fresh plumb raspberries without grainy seeds.

2 cups raspberries
³/₄ cup finely chopped
    rhubarb
2 tablespoons lemon juice
¹/₄ cup water
³/₄ cup sugar

SERVES 4

Purée raspberries and rhubarb in blender. Combine lemon juice, water and sugar in a saucepan. Stir over low heat until sugar is dissolved. Mix in raspberry-rhubarb purée, and simmer 15 minutes.

Pour into 8-inch square pan, set in freezer. Using rubber spatula, stir every 15 minutes until creamy, about 2 hours, then cover and allow to freeze. To serve, scoop into small dishes and garnish with fruit.

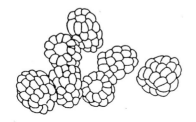

Serving: 1/4 Recipe
Calories from Fat: 3
Saturated Fat: 0 gm
Component of Fat: 1%

Calories: 182
Total Fat: .5 gm
Carbs: 46 gm
Cholesterol: 0 mg

Protein: 1 gm
Dietary Fiber: 3 gm
Sodium: 2 mg
Calcium: 34 mg

The early American settlers created herbal gardens for cooking, medicine and cosmetics. These colonial gardens were enclosed with wattle fences, made from young saplings woven together. As with modern methods of companion planting, herbs, flowers and vegetables were intermixed to create natural protective barriers from pests.

Honey-Carrot Cake

SERVES 12

1 cup honey
$^1/_2$ cup packed brown sugar
$1^1/_4$ cups water
1 cup raisins
$2^1/_2$ cups packed finely
    grated carrots
3 tablespoons canola oil
1 teaspoon cinnamon
$^1/_4$ teaspoon cloves
$^1/_4$ teaspoon nutmeg
$^1/_2$ cup chopped nuts
2 cups all-purpose flour
2 teaspoons baking
    powder
1 teaspoon baking soda

In a saucepan, combine honey, brown sugar, water, raisins, carrots, oil and spices. Bring to a boil, then reduce heat and simmer 8 minutes. Cover saucepan and chill 3 hours.

In a mixing bowl, combine nuts, flour, baking powder and baking soda. After the cooked carrot mixture has chilled 3 hours, briefly stir in flour mixture, mixing just enough to moisten. Pour into 9" x 9" cake pan, sprayed with non-stick vegetable oil. Bake in 275° oven 60 minutes, or until toothpick inserted in center comes out clean.

Serving: 1/12 Cake	Calories: 298	Protein: 4 gm
Calories from Fat: 61	Total Fat: 6.5 gm	Dietary Fiber: 2 gm
Saturated Fat: .5 gm	Carbs: 59 gm	Sodium: 187 mg
Component of Fat: 19%	Cholesterol: 0 mg	Calcium: 60 mg

Colonial gardens produced herbs that were bunched and dried for the winter, or hung near doorways to ward off evil spirits (and mosquitoes.) Herbs commonly grown by the early settlers include basil, caraway, dill, feverfew, marigold, parsley, thyme, pennyroyal, chervil, comfrey, lemon balm, sweet cicely, lovage and valerian.

Strawberry Shortcake

2 cups all-purpose flour
1 tablespoon baking
    powder
2 tablespoons sugar
4 tablespoons unsalted
    butter, chilled
$^1/_4$ cup canola oil, chilled
1 cup cold skim milk
flour for rolling dough

1 quart strawberries,
    cleaned and halved
$^1/_2$ cup sugar

Whipped cream or low-fat
    substitute

SERVES 9

Place oven rack on center shelf. Preheat oven to 400°. Mix together flour, baking powder and a tablespoon of the sugar. Use a pair of butter knives or a pastry cutter to cut butter and oil into flour mixture. Take a fork and stir in milk until just moistened. Let dough rest while lightly flouring your rolling surface.

Lightly roll dough into 6" x 10" rectangle. Fold 6-inch sides into the center, then fold in half. Roll again and repeat folding process. Gently roll dough to 9" x 9". Cut into 9 squares. Place on ungreased cookie sheet 2-inches apart. Sprinkle tops with remaining tablespoon of sugar. Bake 10-11 minutes.

Mix strawberries and one-quarter cup sugar. Let set for 30 minutes. Slice shortcakes into tops and bottoms. Layer strawberries between sliced shortcakes. Serve with whipped cream.

Serving: 1 Shortcake	Calories: 266	Protein: 4 gm
Calories from Fat: 97	Total Fat: 11 gm	Dietary Fiber: 2 gm
Saturated Fat: 3 gm	Carbs: 39 gm	Sodium: 149 mg
Component of Fat: 36%	Cholesterol: 11 mg	Calcium: 106 mg

Old-Fashioned Molasses Cookies

$^{1}/_{2}$ cup softened butter
$^{1}/_{2}$ cup sugar
1 egg
$^{1}/_{2}$ cup molasses
$^{1}/_{2}$ cup low-fat buttermilk
$2^{1}/_{2}$ cups sifted cake flour
1 teaspoon baking soda
1 teaspoon cinnamon
1 teaspoon powdered
     ginger
pinch of salt

MAKES 4 DOZEN COOKIES

Preheat oven to 350°. Spray cookie sheet with non-stick vegetable oil.

Cream butter and sugar together. Beat in egg and molasses, then the buttermilk.

In a separate bowl, sift together remaining ingredients. Keeping batter smooth, slowly beat dry ingredients into the wet mixture.

Drop batter by heaping teaspoon onto cookie sheet. Bake 8-10 minutes. Cookies are very soft while hot, so cool 2 minutes before removing from pan.

Serving: 2 Cookies	Calories: 114	Protein: 1 gm
Calories from Fat: 40	Total Fat: 4.5 gm	Dietary Fiber: 0 gm
Saturated Fat: 2.5 gm	Carbs: 17 gm	Sodium: 114 mg
Component of Fat: 34%	Cholesterol: 20 mg	Calcium: 58 mg

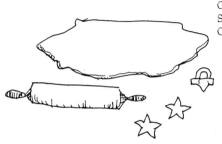

Easter Cutter Cookies

$\frac{1}{2}$ cup brown sugar
$\frac{1}{2}$ cup softened butter
1 teaspoon vanilla
2 eggs
$2\frac{1}{2}$ cups sifted all-
    purpose flour
2 teaspoons double-acting
    baking powder
pinch of salt
flour for rolling

When cutter cookies have cooled, decorate them with Fluffy Fat-Free Icing.

MAKES 3 DOZEN 2-INCH COOKIES

Cream together sugar and butter. Beat in remaining ingredients. Cover and refrigerate dough for 3-4 hours.

Preheat oven to 350°. Spray cookie sheet with non-stick vegetable oil. Handle the dough as little as possible and use very little flour in the rolling process (try using a pastry cloth or pin cover). As needed, sprinkle flour on surface and rub on rolling pin to keep from sticking. Roll dough evenly, about $\frac{1}{4}$-inch thick. Press out shapes with cookie cutters and decorate with sugar and/or cinnamon. Place on cookie sheet and bake 7-12 minutes.

Serving: 2 Cookies	Calories: 138	Protein: 2 gm
Calories from Fat: 55	Total Fat: 6 gm	Dietary Fiber: 0 gm
Saturated Fat: 3.5 gm	Carbs: 18 gm	Sodium: 116 mg
Component of Fat: 40%	Cholesterol: 38 mg	Calcium: 30 mg

FLUFFY FAT-FREE ICING: Combine 3 tablespoons boiling water with 1 cup confectioner's sugar. In a separate bowl, use electric beaters to whip 1 egg white and $\frac{1}{4}$ teaspoon cream of tarter. Add hot syrup to egg white and whip at high speed for 4 minutes, while adding half-a-teaspoon vanilla. To color, stir in a couple drops of food coloring.

Maple Cream Pudding

3 cups skimmed
    evaporated milk
1 cup maple syrup
2 tablespoons cornstarch
2 eggs, beaten
nutmeg (optional)

SERVES 4

Boil water in bottom pan of double boiler. In a separate pot, scald 2¾ cups of the evaporated milk with the maple syrup, then pour into the top pan of the double boiler.

In a small bowl, blend remaining milk with cornstarch. Stirring constantly, slowly add cornstarch mixture to scalded milk. Continue stirring and cook (in top pan of double boiler) over boiling water 20 minutes.

Remove ¹/₂-cup pudding, cool, and whisk in eggs. Stirring constantly, mix back into pudding and cook 5 minutes more. Pour into bowls and if desired, sprinkle with nutmeg. Chill until firm.

Serving: 1/4 Recipe	Calories: 398	Protein: 18 gm
Calories from Fat: 28	Total Fat: 3 gm	Dietary Fiber: 0 gm
Saturated Fat: 1 gm	Carbs: 76 gm	Sodium: 260 mg
Component of Fat: 7%	Cholesterol: 113 mg	Calcium: 648 mg

Plum Pudding

Warm the Plum Pudding and serve with Hot Wine Sauce for a delicious, traditional dessert. This is very rich, and small pieces are plenty filling.

$^1/_2$ cup softened butter
1 cup sugar
2 eggs
2 egg whites
1 cup raisins
1 cup dried currants
$^1/_3$ cup chopped pecans
2 tablespoons flour
2 cups plain breadcrumbs
2 teaspoons cinnamon
$^1/_2$ teaspoon cloves
$^1/_2$ teaspoon allspice

SERVES 12

Preheat oven to 375°. Cream butter and sugar. Beat in eggs and whites one at a time. In a separate bowl, dust raisins, currants and pecans with flour. Stir into the wet mixture.

Mix breadcrumbs and spices, stir into wet mixture. Pour into small baking dish sprayed with non-stick oil. Bake 30 minutes.

Serving: 1/12 Recipe	Calories: 267	Protein: 4 gm
Calories from Fat: 103	Total Fat: 11.5 gm	Dietary Fiber: 2 gm
Saturated Fat: 5.5 gm	Carbs: 41 gm	Sodium: 144 mg
Component of Fat: 37%	Cholesterol: 57 mg	Calcium: 40 mg

Hot Wine Sauce

MAKES $2^1/_4$ CUPS

2 tablespoons butter
1 tablespoon lemon juice
$1^1/_4$ cup sugar
2 eggs
$1^1/_2$ cups sherry or Madeira

Cream butter, lemon juice and sugar. Beat in eggs, then the wine. Just before serving, boil water in lower pan of double boiler. Beat sauce in upper pan until thickened.

Serving: 3 Tablespoons	Calories: 151	Protein: 1 gm
Calories from Fat: 26	Total Fat: 3 gm	Dietary Fiber: 0 gm
Saturated Fat: 1.5 gm	Carbs: 23 gm	Sodium: 32 mg
Component of Fat: 17%	Cholesterol: 41 mg	Calcium: 7 mg

Cheesecake with Glazed Pears

Cheesecake Crust:
2 cups low-fat honey
    graham cracker crumbs
2 tablespoons canola oil

Cheesecake Filling:
2 eggs
16 oz. softened non-fat
    cream cheese
1 cup non-fat sour cream
2 teaspoons cornstarch
$^3/_4$ cup sugar
2 teaspoons vanilla extract

Glazed Pears:
4 pears, peeled and halved
$^1/_4$ cup sugar
1 teaspoon cornstarch
2 tablespoons brandy

MAKES ONE 9-INCH CHEESECAKE

Combine crust ingredients in mixing bowl. Spray 9-inch spring mold pan with non-stick vegetable spray. Press cracker mixture into pan and $2^1/_2$ inches up sides. Bake in 375° oven 3 minutes, then chill.

In blender, whip eggs, cream cheese and sour cream. Transfer to bowl, add remaining filling ingredients. Beat until smooth, then pour into crust. Bake on upper rack at 325° for 30 minutes. Chill 6 hours before glazing.

Boil $^1/_2$-cup water in medium saucepan. Add pear halves, cover pan, reduce heat and cook 10 minutes. Remove pears with slotted spoon. Stir sugar into hot pear juice and boil. Mix cornstarch with 1 tablespoon cold water, stir into syrup until thickened. Remove from heat and add brandy. Arrange pears on cheesecake, pour glaze evenly over all. Chill.

Serving: 1/8 Cheesecake
Calories from Fat: 56
Saturated Fat: 1.5 gm
Component of Fat: 17%

Calories: 327
Total Fat: 6 gm
Carbs: 54 gm
Cholesterol: 58 mg

Protein: 13 gm
Dietary Fiber: 2 gm
Sodium: 397 mg
Calcium: 163 mg

Toffee Taffy

*Be sure to place these candies in a tightly covered tin
and they'll become incredibly smooth and creamy.*

2¹/₂ cups sugar
¹/₂ cup water
4 tablespoons skim milk
4 teaspoons butter
1¹/₂ teaspoons vanilla
    extract or rum
¹/₄ cup powdered sugar

MAKES ABOUT 1 POUND

Over low heat stir sugar, water, milk and butter, until sugar is completely dissolved. Turn heat up to moderate. Without stirring, heat to about 265° on a candy thermometer. Spray a marble slab or ceramic platter with non-stick oil. Holding pan facing away from you and close to the slab, carefully and slowly pour hot liquid onto prepared surface. (Don't let it splatter you.) Let cool until pressing on taffy produces a dent.

Gather taffy into a lump. Using fingertips, pull it into 18-inch strips, fold in half, and then pull again. Continue pulling, folding and twisting taffy while working in vanilla or rum. After 15 minutes, taffy will become porous, opaque, firm and satiny. Roll into a ball and cover with powdered sugar. Pull taffy into 1-inch strips, and cut with oiled shears into individual pieces. Makes about 70 pieces.

To Store: Dust individual candies in powdered sugar and place in tightly covered tin for 12 hours. Wrap in foil and store in a tin.

Serving: 5 Pieces	Calories: 159	Protein: 0 gm
Calories from Fat: 11	Total Fat: 1 gm	Dietary Fiber: 0 gm
Saturated Fat: .5 gm	Carbs: 38 gm	Sodium: 15 mg
Component of Fat: 6%	Cholesterol: 3 mg	Calcium: 6 mg

Seasonal

Preserves & Jams

CONTENTS

ABOUT CANNING

Jars: Use only properly sealed canning jars with rubber airtight seals or a two-piece metal screw-down lid. Check against defects such as chips or cracks. Jars must be sterilized in boiling water or dishwasher, and filled while still hot.

Packing Jars: Fill while preserves and jar are very hot, leaving $1/4$ to $1/2$-inch headroom. Before sealing, release trapped air by running a butter knife or spatula down the insides of the jar. Wipe top of jar clean before sealing.

Canning at a High Altitude: Increase processing time in boiling water bath by 1 minute for every 1000 feet above sea level.

Strawberry Jam

1 quart ripe strawberries,
   cleaned, hulled and
   cut in half
3 cups sugar
1 pouch (3 oz.) liquid fruit
   pectin
1 tablespoon lemon juice

MAKES 2 PINTS

Wash and hull berries. Spray heavy 10-inch pot with non-stick oil. Put strawberries in pot and cover with sugar. Set on low heat and stir gently. When the strawberries begin to juice, mix in fruit pectin.

Increase the heat to moderate, and stop stirring. When strawberries start boiling, set the timer for 15 minutes, and do not disturb. Remove from heat, sprinkle with lemon juice. Allow uncovered strawberries to cool.

Stir lightly and pack in hot sterilized jars. Seal according to manufacturer's directions.

Serving: 2 Tablespoons   Calories: 93   Protein: 0 gm
Calories from Fat: 1   Total Fat: 0 gm   Dietary Fiber: 0 gm
Saturated Fat: 0 gm   Carbs: 23 gm   Sodium: 0 mg
Component of Fat: 1%   Cholesterol: 0 mg   Calcium: 3 mg

Raspberry Jelly

3 cups ripe raspberries
1 teaspoon lemon juice
1 cup sugar
1 pouch (3 oz.) liquid
    fruit pectin

MAKES 2 JELLY JARS

Crush raspberries, add lemon juice and cook in covered saucepan over medium heat for 20 minutes. Remove from heat and strain through a jelly bag. Squeeze well.

Return juice to saucepan and add sugar and pectin. Bring to a full boil for 3 minutes.

Pour into hot sterilized jelly jars. Seal according to manufacturer's directions.

Serving: 2 Tablespoons	Calories: 89	Protein: 0 gm
Calories from Fat: 1	Total Fat: 0 gm	Dietary Fiber: 2 gm
Saturated Fat: 0 gm	Carbs: 21 gm	Sodium: 0 mg
Component of Fat: 1%	Cholesterol: 0 mg	Calcium: 5 mg

Raspberries were commonly cultivated in New England by the mid-1700's. Cold-tolerant raspberry bushes will withstand winter temperatures of 30° below zero. These sweet, late spring and early summer berries come in shades of red, pink, purple and light golden yellow. You can even purchase seedless varieties and raspberry bushes without thorns.

Ginger-Rhubarb Conserve

1 orange
1 lemon
$^1/_2$ cup water
$^1/_4$ cup vinegar
3 cups sugar
$^1/_4$ cup golden raisins
2 tablespoons fresh
    grated ginger
2 whole cloves
$^1/_2$ teaspoon mace
$1^1/_2$ cups rhubarb, cleaned
    and finely chopped

MAKES 8 JELLY JARS
Read about canning on page 150.

Seed the orange and lemon. Scoop pulp into saucepan, add water, vinegar, sugar, raisins and ginger. Boil. Tie spices in a cheesecloth, and simmer in the syrup 5 minutes. Stir in rhubarb, cook until thickened. Pack and seal in sterilized jars, leaving $^1/_2$ inch headroom.

Place jars on rack in boiler half-filled with boiling water, leaving space between jars. Add boiling water to cover jars 2 inches above their tops. Bring to a boil, cover, and process 10 minutes. Using tongs, lift jars (not by the lids) and set on towels with several inches between them to cool.

Serving: 1/4 Cup	Calories: 80	Protein: 0 gm
Calories from Fat: 0	Total Fat: 0 gm	Dietary Fiber: 1 gm
Saturated Fat: 0 gm	Carbs: 21 gm	Sodium: 1 mg
Component of Fat: 0%	Cholesterol: 0 mg	Calcium: 12 mg

Strawberry and Pineapple Preserve

1 quart cleaned and
    hulled strawberries
2 cups sugar
1 cup canned unsweetened
    crushed pineapple,
    well drained
1 teaspoon lemon zest
2 teaspoons lemon juice

MAKES 2 PINTS

Combine all ingredients in saucepan. Stirring frequently, simmer uncovered for 20 minutes. When thickened, pack mixture into hot sterilized jars.

Will keep in the refrigerator about 2 weeks. You can also seal the jars with a two-piece metal screw-down lid, following the manufacturer's instructions. Store in a cool dark place.

Serving: 2 Tablespoons	Calories: 56	Protein: 0 gm
Calories from Fat: 1	Total Fat: 0 gm	Dietary Fiber: 0 gm
Saturated Fat: 0 gm	Carbs: 14 gm	Sodium: 0 mg
Component of Fat: 1%	Cholesterol: 0 mg	Calcium: 3 mg

Hot Pepper Jelly

1 cup finely chopped
    green pepper
1-2 finely chopped
    jalapeno peppers
$^3/_4$ cup cider vinegar
2 cups sugar
$^1/_2$ teaspoon white pepper
pinch of salt
3 oz. liquid pectin

MAKES 3 JELLY JARS

Purée both peppers and vinegar in blender or food processor until smooth. Pour into saucepan and stir in sugar, white pepper and salt. Bring to a full boil. Remove from heat. Rest for 5 minutes, then skim off foam. Add pectin and pour into hot sterilized jelly jars.

Will keep in refrigerator 2 weeks. You can also process as jelly and seal with a two-piece metal screw-down lid, according to manufacturer's instructions.

Serving: 2 Tablespoons	Calories: 88	Protein: 0 gm
Calories from Fat: 0	Total Fat: 0 gm	Dietary Fiber: 0 gm
Saturated Fat: 0 gm	Carbs: 22 gm	Sodium: 29 mg
Component of Fat: 0%	Cholesterol: 0 mg	Calcium: 4 mg

When working with hot peppers, remember they contain oils that can cause painful burns to sensitive skin. Do not rub your eyes, nose, mouth, or face before thoroughly washing your hands. Also, children's skin is especially delicate and can be hurt by hot pepper oils. Some cooks prefer to wear rubber gloves to work with hot peppers and seeds.

Pickled Dill Beans

2 lbs. tender green or
  yellow beans
4 pinches cayenne pepper
4 cloves crushed garlic
4 teaspoons dill seed
$2^1/_2$ cups water
$2^1/_2$ cups vinegar
2 tablespoons salt

MAKES 4 PINTS
Read about canning on page 150.

Pack beans lengthwise in hot sterile jars. To each pint jar, add one-quarter of the cayenne, garlic and dill seed. Boil remaining ingredients together, pour over beans and spices, leaving $^1/_4$-inch headroom. Seal jars.

Place jars on rack in boiler half-filled with boiling water, leaving space between jars. Add boiling water to cover jars 2 inches above their tops. Bring to a boil, cover, and process 10 minutes. Using tongs, lift jars (not by the lids) and set on towels with several inches between them to cool.

Serving: 1/2 Cup	Calories: 27	Protein: 1 gm
Calories from Fat: 2	Total Fat: 0 gm	Dietary Fiber: 2 gm
Saturated Fat: 0 gm	Carbs: 7 gm	Sodium: 439 mg
Component of Fat: 6%	Cholesterol: 0 mg	Calcium: 39 mg

Sweet & Sour Pickles

5 lbs. small pickling
    cucumbers, scrubbed
$^1/_4$ cup pickling salt
boiling water
3 cups water
4 cups cider vinegar
2 cups sugar
2 tablespoons whole
    mixed pickling spices
6-inches broken
    cinnamon sticks
1 teaspoon whole cloves

MAKES 6 PINTS
Read about canning on page 150.

Cover cucumbers with cold water mixed with pickling salt. Soak 24 hours, then drain. Briefly cover cucumbers with boiling water, drain, then pack into sterilized jars. Boil 3 cups water with remaining ingredients. Fill jars with boiling vinegar mixture. Seal jars.

Place jars on rack in boiler half-filled with boiling water, leaving space between jars. Add boiling water to cover jars 2 inches above their tops. Boil, cover, and process 15 minutes. Using tongs, lift jars and set on towels with several inches between them to cool.

Serving: 1/4 Cup	Calories: 42	Protein: 0 gm
Calories from Fat: 1	Total Fat: 0 gm	Dietary Fiber: 0 gm
Saturated Fat: 0 gm	Carbs: 11 gm	Sodium: 50 mg
Component of Fat: 2%	Cholesterol: 0 mg	Calcium: 10 mg

Most of the older New England homesteads had root cellars for preserving vegetables and fruits. Today's root cellars provide an inexpensive way to extend the useful life of our own homegrown produce. Successful storage requires a temperature between 32° and 40°, with a high humidity level ranging from 60% to 70%.

Yankee Chutney

While you're waiting for green tomatoes to ripen, try this great chutney.

12 green tomatoes
12 apples, peeled and
    cored
3 peeled onions
4 cups vinegar
1 cup red wine
3 cups sugar
1 teaspoon cayenne
    pepper
2 teaspoons powdered
    ginger
1 teaspoon turmeric
2 cloves crushed garlic
1 teaspoon salt

MAKES 8 PINTS
Read about canning on page 150.

Chop tomatoes, apples and onions. In a large saucepan, bring all other ingredients to a boil, then add the chopped items and simmer together 1 hour. Pack in hot sterilized jars, leaving $\frac{1}{2}$-inch headroom. Seal jars.

Place jars on rack in boiler half-filled with boiling water, leaving space between jars. Add enough boiling water to cover jars 2 inches above their tops. Bring to a boil, cover, and process 10 minutes. Using tongs, lift jars (not by the lids) and set on towels with several inches between them to cool.

Serving: 1/4 Cup	Calories: 63	Protein: 0 gm
Calories from Fat: 1	Total Fat: 0 gm	Dietary Fiber: 1 gm
Saturated Fat: 0 gm	Carbs: 16 gm	Sodium: 40 mg
Component of Fat: 2%	Cholesterol: 0 mg	Calcium: 7 mg

Cucumber Tomato Juice

1 large cucumber
1 quart tomato juice
1 teaspoon olive oil
2 teaspoons vinegar
pinch of basil
pinch of paprika
cracked ice
lemon wedges

SERVES 8

Cut cucumber into cubes, then process in blender. Strain juice into pitcher. Mix in olive oil, vinegar and spices.

Pour Cucumber Tomato Juice over cracked ice in glasses. Serve with lemon wedges.

Serving: 12 oz.	Calories: 40	Protein: 1 gm
Calories from Fat: 6	Total Fat: .5 gm	Dietary Fiber: 0 gm
Saturated Fat: 0 gm	Carbs: 8 gm	Sodium: 196 mg
Component of Fat: 13%	Cholesterol: 0 mg	Calcium: 26 mg

The Coastal New England
Cooking Series

NOTES ON USING THESE BOOKS

Each book is oriented to take advantage of the fresh produce of the season. Try to buy locally grown produce in the freshest condition possible. Locally grown food not only has the best flavor and greatest amount of vitamins, but it is economical as well.

To allow for a variety of foods, fruits and vegetables which freeze or dry well are also used in their preferred state of storage. Fresh produce, fish, grains, flours, dairy and beans provide a diverse and healthy diet, without the animal fats and other problems associated with red meat.

Non-fat and low-fat dairy products are readily available and provide calcium, protein, nutrition and flavor, with much less fat. They are an excellent substitute to whole milk products. Low-sodium tomato products and bouillon broth are occasionally used, substitution of regular items will simply increase sodium.

Non-stick oil spray is intended to mean a non-fat vegetable oil spray. When it is used in addition to a cooking oil, it allows the use of less oil.

The nutritional analysis assumes a "pinch of salt" or "salt to taste" is .05 teaspoons of salt. The same measurement is used for other spices as well.

Preheating the oven or broiler takes only 15 minutes. Save electricity: don't warm your appliances until 15 minutes before they will be used.

Following the Guidelines of
The American Heart Association

A complete statement of the Guidelines of the American Heart Association can be obtained by contacting your local chapter. For healthy adults, this cookbook presents a simple approach to following these guidelines. Adding together the various nutritional components of your meals will help provide a better understanding of your diet.

By reducing meat and chicken, a large amount of saturated fat (an artery-damaging fat) will be replaced by more healthful protein and fats. Saturated fats should be limited to 10% of calories. All animal products, including cheese, also contain cholesterol, and their use should be limited.

Polyunsaturated fats (found in salmon, leafy vegetables and seeds), and especially the Omega-3 fatty acids, are believed to have an anticlotting agent helpful in preventing heart attack and stroke. Monounsaturated fats are often praised for not raising the damaging LDL cholesterol, and are found in olive and canola oils.

Keep the amount of pre-prepared foods to a minimum. Enjoy a wide variety of fresh foods with a broad range of their natural vitamins, minerals and nutrients. Fresh fruits and vegetables can be eaten regularly, without restriction.

Total fat intake should not exceed 30% of the calories consumed. Even polyunsaturated and monounsaturated fats should be consumed in limited quantities, and will achieve the greatest benefit if they replace, not supplement, the saturated fats presently consumed.

Following the Guidelines of
The American Heart Association

(cont.) Carbohydrates should make up at least 50-60% of the diet. This includes vegetables, fruits, grains, flours and beans. The American Heart Association recommends calories be adjusted to achieve and maintain a healthy body weight.

Make a habit of reaching for fruit or naturally sweetened products. The recipes in this book offer a reasonable alternative to the traditional high-fat and caloric desserts, but they are not intended to be eaten everyday or in volumes greater than the proportions shown.

Sodium intake should follow the advice of your physician, or be limited to an average of 3 grams per day. Recipes in this book can be made without salt or allow for "salt to taste." The desire for salty foods is acquired, you can become more sensitive to the taste of salt by slowly reducing its volume. Try using sea salt in small amounts, it is more flavorful and contains minerals not present in table salt.

Limit alcohol to a maximum of one or two drinks per day. And...

Exercise! It makes your body work better, and feel better, too.

Suggested Kitchen Tools, Utensils and Stock Items

Kitchen Tools and Utensils:
Set of whisks in assorted sizes
Slotted spoon and spatula
Blender
Double boiler
Non-stick skillet and frying pans in assorted sizes with lids
Oven casseroles with lids
Non-aluminum pots, pans and containers
Rolling pin
Large stainless steel bowl for mixing bread dough
Pie pans, regular and deep-dish

Stock Items:
A good variety of spices, fresh fruits and vegetables
Non-stick, non-fat vegetable oil spray
Canola, olive and safflower oils
Vegetable bouillon cubes or powder
Skim milk
Non-fat powdered milk (to enrich skim milk)
Low-fat buttermilk
Non-fat plain yogurt, cottage cheese and cream cheese
Low-fat and part-skim cheese products

Measurements

a pinch.............................. $^1/_{20}$ teaspoon
3 teaspoons......................... 1 tablespoon
4 tablespoons....................... $^1/_4$ cup
16 tablespoons...................... 1 cup
2 cups............................... 1 pint
4 cups............................... 1 quart
4 quarts............................. 1 gallon
8 quarts............................. 1 peck
16 ounces........................... 1 pound
8 ounces liquid..................... 1 cup
1 ounce liquid...................... 2 tablespoons

Substitutions

1 tablespoon cornstarch........... 2 T. flour or 2 tsp. quick-cooking tapioca
2 teaspoons arrowroot............. 1 tablespoon cornstarch
1 teaspoon baking powder .... $^1/_4$ tsp. baking soda + $^1/_2$ tsp. cream of tartar
$^1/_2$ cup brown sugar................. 2 T. molasses in $^1/_2$ cup granulated sugar
$^3/_4$ cup cracker crumbs............. 1 cup bread crumbs
1 tablespoon fresh herbs.......... 1 teaspoon dried herbs
1 small clove garlic................. $^1/_8$ teaspoon garlic powder
1 fresh onion....................... 2 T. instant minced onion, rehydrated
1 cup whole milk................... $^1/_2$ c. skimmed evaporated milk + $^1/_2$ c. water
1 cup buttermilk................... 1 cup non-fat plain yogurt

PRINTED IN THE U.S.A.

20% TOTAL RECYCLED FIBER
20% POST CONSUMER FIBER

If you enjoy this seasonal cookbook, try the others in the Coastal New England Cooking series. Each book has 170 pages of great New England recipes, historical and culinary trivia, and the original artwork of local artists. Our unique and beautiful covers complement the flavor of this wonderful collection. Cookbooks are also a gift that will be used for years.

_____ *Coastal New England Spring Cooking*...........................$13.95

_____ *Coastal New England Summertime Cooking*.................$13.95

_____ *Coastal New England Fall Harvest Cooking*.................$13.95

_____ *Coastal New England Winterfare & Holiday Cooking*...$13.95

_____ Total Quantity x $13.95......................$_____

Maine Residents add 6% sales tax..........$_____

Shipping Charge: $2.00 first book, $_____
plus $1.00 for each additional book

TOTAL $_____

Please enclose check or money order made payable to:

Harvest Hill Press
P.O. Box 55
Salisbury Cove, Maine 04672

VISA / M.C # _ _ _ _ - _ _ _ _ - _ _ _ _ - _ _ _ _

Expiration Date:_____   Signature_____

For faster service on VISA / Master Card orders, call (207) 288-8900.

Orders paid by personal check shipped within 3 weeks of receipt, all other orders shipped in 3 business days.